VIKING S(

FOR NORTHERN RESEARCH

TEXT SERIES

General Editors
A. R. Faulkes and P. G. Foote

VOLUME VII (ii)

HÁVAMÁL

Edited by David A. H. Evans

GLOSSARY AND INDEX

Compiled by Anthony Faulkes

HÁVAMÁL

EDITED BY DAVID A. H. EVANS

GLOSSARY
AND INDEX

COMPILED BY ANTHONY FAULKES

VIKING SOCIETY

FOR NORTHERN RESEARCH

UNIVERSITY COLLEGE LONDON

PREFACE

Apart from ordinary personal pronouns all words in the *Hávamál* text issued by the Viking Society in 1986 are glossed and all proper names entered in the following list. Except where curtailed by "etc.", references given to the occurrence of a word may be taken to be complete. The appearance of "n" after a reference means that there is comment on the word in the notes of the edition.

I owe warm thanks to Mr Paul Bibire, Cambridge, for typing in my text and preparing the disk from which the Glossary has been set.

Anthony Faulkes

ABBREVIATIONS

a.	adjective	*neg.*	negative
abs(ol).	absolute(ly)	*nom.*	nominative
acc.	accusative	*num.*	numeral
adv.	adverb(ial)	*obj.*	object
art.	article	*OE*	Old English
aux.	auxiliary	*ord.*	ordinal
comp.	comparative	*o-self*	oneself
conj.	conjunction	*p.*	past
dat.	dative	*pers.*	person
def.	definite	*pl.*	plural
e-m	einhverjum	*poss.*	possessive
e-n	einhvern	*pp.*	past participle
e-s	einhvers	*prep.*	preposition(al)
e-t	eitthvat	*pres. (p.)*	present participle
e-u	einhverju	*pret. pres.*	preterite-present
f.	feminine	*pron.*	pronoun
gen.	genitive	*rel.*	relative
imp.	imperative	*sg.*	singular
impers.	impersonal	*s-one*	someone
indecl.	indeclinable	*s-thing*	something
inf.	infinitive	*subj.*	subjunctive
interrog.	interrogative	*subst.*	substantive
intrans.	intransitive	*sup.*	superlative
irreg.	irregular	*sv.*	strong verb
m.	masculine	*trans.*	transitive
md.	middle voice	*vb(s).*	verb(s)
n.	neuter	*wv.*	weak verb

-a *neg. suffix* used with vbs. 11/5 12/1 22/6 27/7 30/2 31/4 35/2 38/2 52/2 75/1 124/6 150/4 158/6; combined with suffixed 1st pers. pron. 39/1 150/5 152/5; with preceding *ne* 135/5. Cf. **-at, -t.**

á (1) pres. of **eiga** 9/2 25/6 26/3 55/6 59/2 62/6.

á (2) *prep.* (1) with dat. 'on' 1/7 2/5 34/3 38/5 41/3 83/2 84/4 89/2 90/4 116/5 138/7 157/2, postposition 35/6 38/2 50/2 ('in'?) 97/2 101/6 105/2 111/2 138/2 154/5; 'on to' 19/1; 'in' 3/3, postposition 155/3; 'at' 83/6; 'on, in' (activity) 112/6, 154/3; 'on, by using' 151/3; of time, 'in the course of' 74/6,7.

(2) with acc. 'to' 59/3 107/6 135/6; 'on' 82/2, 'into, at' 62/3; 'on to' 136/6, postposition 158/3 (with *þegn*); abstractly: 'to' 111/6, 'into' 102/6, 'upon' 93/4,5 82/5,6 (to be understood also in lines 7 and 8, see **orka**).

(3) as adv. 'in it, about this' 108/1.

abbindi *n.* 'tenesmus, useless straining of the bowels' 137/9.

aðal *n.* 'natural characteristic, distinguishing feature' 103/9.

áðr *conj.* 'before' 1/2.

af *prep.* with dat. 'from, off' 21/3 44/3 45/3 57/1,3,4,6 117/8 123/1 138/9 140/2 141/4,6 149/6,7; 'because of, through' 69/3,4,5,6 75/3 150/2. As adv. 'from her' 130/7.

afglapi *m.* 'fool' 17/1.

afhvarf *n.* 'indirect route, roundabout way' 34/1.

afl *n.* 'strength' 160/4.

aka (ók) *sv.* with dat. 'drive' 90/3 ('as if one were to drive', 'like driving').

akr *m.* **(-rs)** '(corn)field' 88/1,4.

ala (ól) *sv.* 'nourish, foster' 48/3; pp. *alinn* 'produced, born' 72/2.

ald- see **ǫld.**

aldinn *a.* 'aged, ancient' 62/3 104/1.

aldregi *adv.* 'never' 6/8 76/5 79/5 93/3 115/6 117/6,9 121/6 122/6 123/2 128/6 132/6 134/6.

aldri *adv.* 'never' 77/5.

aldrtregi *m.* 'life-sorrow' 20/3n.

álfr *m.* 'elf' 143/2 159/4 160/5.

allr *a. pron.* 'all, every' 1/1 23/6 24/2 25/2 53/4 100/3 159/5; '(the) whole (of)' 23/2 51/6 99/6 121/10 124/3 138/3 154/6 161/3,5; *þessu ǫllu* '(in) all this' 89/8; *ǫllum* 'for or to everyone' 136/3 153/2; n. 'everything, it all' 17/4 26/2 163/4, with pl. vb. and complement 98/4 (or as adv., 'altogether'), 'anything' 124/4; gen. n. as adv. 'entirely' 69/1.

allþarfr *a.* 'very needful, useful' (*e-m* 'to, for s-one') 164/3 (referring to *mál*).

alskjótr *a.* 'absolutely fast, the very fastest' 89/4 ('a horse at maximum speed'?).

alsnotr *a.* 'completely wise' 55/6.

án *prep.* 'without'; with inf., *án at lifa* 'without living' 68/6.

andskoti *m.* 'opponent, enemy' 148/5.

ann pres. of **unna**.

annarr *pron. a. and ord. num.* 'another (person)' 8/6 9/6 30/2 35/6 45/1 47/5 58/2 65/2 75/5 93/3 94/2 115/5 124/6 131/8; 'a second (person)' 63/5; *þat ... annat* 'this second one' (*ljóð*) 147/1.

api *m.* 'ape, fool' 75/3 122/7.

aptann *m.* 'evening' 98/1.

aptr *adv.* 'back' 14/5 99/1 104/2 139/6 145/9.

ár *adv.* 'early' 58/1 59/1.

árliga *adv.* 'early (in the day)' 33/1.

armr *m.* 'arm' 108/6 163/8.

ársáinn *a.* (*pp.*) 'sown early (in the year)' 88/1.

áss *m.* (pl. **æsir**) 'one of the race of gods associated with Óðinn' 143/1 159/4 160/4.

ást *f.* 'love' 92/3 93/1.

Ásviðr *m.* 143/4.

-at *neg. suffix* with vbs. 10/2 11/2 30/5 50/3 69/1 114/4 133/4 146/2 152/4 158/4; with imp. 112/5 127/7; followed by suffixed 2nd pers. pron. *skalattu* 'you shall not' 113/6 125/6 129/6. Cf. **-a, -t**.

at (1) *prep.* with acc. 'after, in memory of' 72/6.

at (2) *adv.* with comp. *at heldr* 'the more (for that)' 96/6.

at (3) *conj.* 'that' 110/2 138/1, 'so that'? 162/2; correlative with *svá* 39/3,6 89/8 100/2 114/2 133/5,6 149/5 150/5 152/5 155/5 157/6, with *þat* 25/6 27/3,5 64/6 131/10, with *því* 14/5, with *þess* 19/6, with *hitt* 22/6 99/5, with *ifi* 108/2. As rel. particle (?) *einn at* 77/5 ('one thing of such a kind that', 'of one thing that it'). Cf. **því at**.

at (4) *particle* with inf. 1/5 19/6 38/4 41/6 54/5 68/6 95/6 97/6 111/1 114/6 124/5 152/6 153/3 154/3; indicating purpose 44/6 109/3 119/7.

at (5) *prep.* with dat. 'at' 22/3 31/3 32/3 67/3 134/5, 'at' or 'for' 136/3, postposition 111/3,9; 'to' 25/5, postposition 61/2; 'into' 120/6 130/6, 'on to' 149/3; 'along' (postposition) 10/2 11/2n 11/5; 'on, in' (postposition) 49/2; 'in, with' 19/2; 'subject to, the object of' 5/4 30/1 132/5, 'the cause of' 118/5 121/7, see **vera (2), verða, hafa**; 'so as to be' (postposition) 115/7; 'about' 23/3

46/3 80/2 109/5; 'with regard to' (or 'in'?) 6/1n 6/3 57/5 117/7 (or 'from, arising from'?) 123/6, 'with' 116/7 (see **fá (2)**) 128/7; 'as' (postposition) 127/6 (see **kveða**); of time, 'to' 23/5, 'in, at' 81/1; elliptically with gen. 'at (the house of), at s-one's' 14/3 67/5.

átjándi *ord. num.* 'eighteenth' 163/1.

átt 2nd pers. sg. pres. of **eiga**.

átti *ord. num.* 'eighth' 153/1.

auðigr *a.* 'wealthy, rich' 47/4 70/5 75/4.

auðr *m.* 'wealth' 10/4 59/6 78/4.

auga *n.* 'eye' 7/5 82/4.

augabragð *n.* 'wink, sidelong glance'; *verða at augabragði, hafa e-n at augabragði* 'become, make s-one, an object of mockery' 5/4 30/1; 'a twinkling of an eye' (i.e. it lasts no longer) 78/5.

auk *adv.* 'also, again' 98/1.

aurum dat. pl. of **eyrir**.

ausa (jós) *sv.* 'pour, ladle (*e-u* from something)'; pp. 140/6n.

ax *n.* 'ear of corn' 137/10.

báðir *a. pron.* 'both'; n. *bæði* (i.e. 'both men and women') 91/2.

band *n.* 'band, bond' 149/3. Cf. **bǫnd**.

bani *m.* 'death' 15/6; 'cause of death (*e-s* to s-thing)' 73/2.

bára *f.* 'wave' 86/2.

barn *n.* 'child' 15/2 86/8.

barr *n.* 'needles (of a conifer), foliage' 50/3.

baugeiðr *m.* 'ring-oath' 110/1n.

baugr *m.* '(arm-)ring' 136/4.

bautarsteinn *m.* 'memorial stone' 72/4n.

baztr, **beztr** *a. sup.* 'best' 68/1; n. 27/3; n. as subst. or adv. *hefir hann bazt* 'it will be best for him, he will do best' 80/6; n. as adv. 48/2.

beðmál *n. pl.* 'bed-talk' 86/5.

beðr *m.* 'bed'; in pl. (but referring to only one bed) 97/2 101/6.

beitta (tt) *wv.* 'tack, beat (against the wind)' (the ship in dat.) 90/8 ('or (as if one) should beat').

beiti *m.* 'earth-worm' 137/13n.

belgr *m.* 'skin, (skin-)bag' 134/8n.

bera (bar) *sv.* 'carry' 78/3; with suffixed neg. *-at* 10/2 11/2; 'bring, put, place' 149/2; pp. *borinn* 'carried (up or in)' 100/5n.

berr *a.* 'bare'; n. as adv. (or subst.) 'plainly, openly' (or 'what is plain, open') 91/1.

Bestla *f.* 140/3.

betri *a. comp.* 'better' 10/1 11/1 71/4 72/1; *inn betri* 'the better person' 125/7; n. *betra* 36/1,6 37/1 163/4, with dat., 'better than' 10/4; *betra er* 'it is better (that it should be)' 145/1,4; *betra er e-m* '(it) is better for s-one' 70/1 124/4n.

beztr *a. sup.* see **baztr**.

bíða (beið) *sv.* 'suffer' 15/6; 'endure, last long enough (continue? achieve, manage?)' 41/6.

biðja (bað) *sv.* 'ask, beg (*e-s* for s-thing, *e-m* for s-one, *sér* for o-self)' 37/5; abs. 'pray, invoke' 144/5; 'wish, invoke, call down (s-thing on s-one)' 136/5; *þá er þér bǫls beðit* 'then evil will be called down upon you, s-one will wish you evil' 126/10. With acc. and inf. 'bid s-one do s-thing' 131/5.

bila (að) *wv.* 'flag, give way, fail' 125/7.

Billingr *m.* 97/1.

binda (batt) *sv.* 'bind, tie (up)' 101/6.

bíta (beit) *sv.* 'bite, cut, wound, harm'; *b. e-m ofarla* 'cause a wound high up in s-one' 118/1n; with suffixed neg. -*t* 148/6 (*þeim*: dat. of advantage, 'for them').

bitsótt *f.* 'sickness, illness caused by a bite or sting' 137/13.

bjarga (barg) *sv.* with dat. 'save' 154/3; with suffixed 1st pers. pron., suffixed neg. and additional 1st pers. pron. 152/5 (*honum* = the hall).

bjóða (bauð, boðinn) *sv.* 'invite, offer (*e-m e-t* s-one s-thing) 92/2; impers. passive *myndi mér boðit* 'I would be invited' 67/2.

bjǫrn *m.* 'bear' 86/7.

blanda (að) *wv.* with dat. 'mix; blend, exchange, share?' 44/4; *e-u er blandat* 's-thing is mixed, there is a mixing, combining of (in?) s-thing' 124/1 ('they are blended, i.e. joined, in affinity').

blindr *a.* 'blind'; as subst. 'a blind man, that a man should be blind' 71/4.

blóðugr *a.* 'bloody' 37/4.

blóta (blét) *sv.* 'worship, sacrifice' 144/6.

bogi *m.* 'bow' 85/1 (dat. dependent upon *trúi* 88/2, like all the datives in between).

bóglimar *m. pl.* 'limbs, arms and legs'; *at bóglimum mér* 'on my arms and legs' 149/3n.

borinn pp. of **bera**.

bráðr *a.* 'hasty, impatient' 2/4n; n. as adv. *brátt* 'quickly, soon' 153/6.

brandr *m.* 'piece of firewood' 57/1; *á brǫndum* '(sitting) on a pile of firewood' 2/5n.

braut *f.* 'road, way' 10/2 11/2 34/3 72/5 89/2.

breiðr *a.* 'broad'; *n.* as adv. 'broadly, extensively' 152/4.

brenna (1) (brann), *pres.* **brenn** or **brennr** *sv.* intrans. 'burn' 51/2 57/2; *b. upp* 'flame up' 70/4; with suffixed neg. *-at* 152/4 ('it will not burn'); pres. p. 85/2 100/4.

brenna (2) (d) *wv.* trans. 'burn, cremate' 71/5 81/2.

bresta (brast) *sv.* 'break'; pres. p. 'breaking' (or 'twanging'? 'breakable'?) 85/1.

brigð *f.* 'changeableness, inconstancy' 84/6.

brigðr *a.* 'changeable, unreliable, deceptive (*e-m* for someone)' 91/3 ('not to be relied upon by women'); *en sé brigðum at vera* 'than it would be for a man to be unreliable (deceptive), than for one to be unreliable' 124/5n.

brjóst *n. pl.* 'breast' 8/6 9/6 84/6.

bróðurbani *m.* 'one's brother's slayer' 89/1.

brók *f.* (*pl.* **brœkr**) 'breeches' 61/4.

brotinn *a.* (pp. of *brjóta*) 'broken' 86/6.

brotna (að) *wv.* intrans. 'break' 89/6.

brúðr *f.* 'bride, wife' 86/5.

brunninn pp. of **brenna (1)**.

brunnr *m.* 'spring, well' 111/3.

bú *n.* 'dwelling, establishment, farm' 36/1 37/1; *á búi* 'at s-one else's house' 83/6n.

búa (bjó) *sv.* 'live, dwell' 34/3 95/2.

bundit pp. of **binda**.

byrðr *f.* 'burden, load' 10/1 11/1.

byrr *m.* '(sailing-)wind' 90/7.

bæði *n.* of **báðir**.

bœn *f.* 'prayer; begging' 36/6.

bœta (tt) *wv.* 'put right, cure, settle, repair' 153/6.

bǫl *n.* 'evil, trouble, misfortune, harm' 126/10 137/14; 'mischief, malice' 127/5,6.

Bǫlverkr *m.* 109/5.

Bǫlþórr *m.* a giant 140/3.

bǫnd *n. pl.* = the gods 109/6.

bǫrkr *m.* 'bark (of tree)' 50/3.

dagr *m.* 'day' 74/6 81/1 82/4; acc. *fimm daga* 'for five days' 51/3; gen. of a point in time 109/1n.

Dáinn *m.* 143/2.

dauðr (1) *m.* 'death' 70/6n.

dauðr (2) *a.* 'dead'; as subst. 'a dead person' 77/6.

daufr *a.* 'deaf'; as subst. 'a deaf person' 71/3.

Dellingr *m.* 160/3.

deyfa (ð) *wv.* 'dull, (make) blunt' 148/4.

deyja (dó) *sv.* 'die' 76/1,2,3,5 77/1,2,3,5.

dómr *m.* 'judgement, reputation' 77/6.

drekka (drakk) *sv.* 'drink' 12/5 83/1 137/5; subj. (optative) 'let him drink' 19/2; pp. *drukkit* 81/6; 'drunk up, finished' 66/4.

drjúgr *a.* 'lasting, ample, substantial'; n. as adv. 'strongly, without weakening' 79/6.

drykkr *m.* 'drink' 105/3 140/4.

duga (ð) *wv.* 'be of use, serve, be successful or adequate' 71/3; *at einugi dugi* 'that he was good for nothing' 133/6.

dul *f.* 'reserve' or 'folly' 57/6; 'folly' or 'conceit' 79/6.

durum dat. pl. of **dyrr**.

Dvalinn *m.* 143/3.

dvelja (dvalða) *wv.* 'delay, hold up'; *mart dvelr e-n* 'many things will be a hindrance for s-one, much will hold one up' 59/4.

dvergr *m.* 'dwarf' 143/3 160/3.

dyrr *f. pl.* 'doorway' 70/6 160/3.

dýrr *a.* 'precious' 105/3 140/5.

dæll *a.* 'easy (to manage)' 5/3.

dœlskr *a.* 'foolish' 57/6.

dœma (ð) *wv.* 'judge; express opinions (*of* about), discuss' 111/7.

eða *conj.* 'or' 17/3 19/3 etc.; 'or (if)' 67/4 109/7; 'or as if' 90/7,9; 'or who' 163/9; 'or else' 136/5.

ef *conj.* 'if' 4/5 16/3 etc.; 'whether' 109/6; correlative with *þá* 17/5 30/5 80/6 89/6, with *ok* 151/2.

egg *f.* 'edge (of weapon)' 148/4.

ei *adv.* 'not' 39/3.

eiga (á, átta) *pret. pres. vb.* 'have, possess' 8/5 9/2 25/6 29/5 36/4 44/1 45/1 55/6 59/2 62/6 119/5; *eiga sér* 'have for o-self' 26/3.

eigi (1) subj. of **eiga**, sg. 36/4, sg. or pl. 29/5n.

eigi (2) *adv.* 'not' 114/2 131/6.

eignask (að) *wv. md.* 'gain possession of (for o-self)' 79/2.

eik *f.* 'oak' 137/9.

einn *a., num.* and *pron.* (*n.* **eitt**) (1) 'one' 89/6, 'one person' 63/4 124/3 163/5, 'one thing' 77/4, 'one of them' (sc. *ljóð*) 146/4, sc. *lær* 67/6; 'the same' 35/3; *eins* 'of one man' 73/1; *einna* with sup. = 'of all' 64/6; 'a certain' 101/4 118/2.
(2) 'only, alone' 18/1 52/1 95/1, 'nothing but' 124/6; *þeiri einni* 'to that (female) person only, alone' (with *kennik*) 163/7; *einn sér,*

einn saman 'on one's own, all alone' 47/2 95/3, *einir saman* 'they only (only the two people concerned) between themselves' 98/5.

einnhverr *pron. a.* 'someone' 121/10.

einnættr *a.* 'one night old' 86/3.

einugi dat. sg. n. of **engi**, 'for not one thing, for nothing' 133/6.

ekki *pron.* n. of **engi**, 'nothing' 5/5 27/5; 'none, not any' (?) 97/5.

eldr *m.* 'fire' 3/1 68/1 70/4 83/1 137/8; dat. of comparison 'than fire' 51/1.

elli *f.* 'old age' 16/4.

ellipti *ord. num.* 'eleventh' 156/1.

en *conj.* 'but' 16/4 21/4 etc.; 'and' 7/5 42/6 74/7 etc.; 'and yet' 32/3; after comp. 'than' 6/9 36/6 40/6 70/2 95/6 124/5, 'than that' 10/3 11/3,6 71/5 145/2,5; *heldr en* 'rather than, instead of' 151/6.

endrgefandi *m.* (*pl.* -**endr**) 'one who gives again, repeated giver' 41/4.

endrþaga *f.* 'silence in return, reciprocated silence' 4/6n.

engi *pron. a.* (cf. **øngr, ekki, einugi**) 'no, not any' 16/5 19/5 43/5 61/5 88/2 93/2; 'no one' 27/4 56/5 64/6.

enn *adv.* 'further, in addition' 46/1; 'again', i.e. 'back' 101/2 108/2.

eptir *prep.* with acc. 'after' 72/3; as adv. 105/5 see **hafa**.

er (1) *rel. particle* and *conj.* (1) 'who, which' 40/2 62/5 142/5; *sá er, sá ... er, þann er, þeir ... er, því er, hinn (...) er* etc. 8/2 18/2 22/5 etc.; *þeirar er* 'who' or 'whom' 108/6, *þeim ... er* 'about which' 138/8, *þat (...) er* 'what' 8/5 95/2, 'which' 136/2 160/2, *þeiri einni er* 'to that one alone who' 163/8; *hveim er* 'for whoever' 76/6; *þá ... hverr er* 'then ... whoever, whenever anyone' 124/2.

(2) 'when' 17/2 24/6 27/2 etc.; *þá er* 'when' 6/4 125/8; correlative with *þá* 23/5 25/5 51/5 64/5 96/2 101/2 102/5 etc.; *opt ... er* 20/5; *þar ... er* 'where' 145/9; *fœra ... er fleira* 'the less ... the more' 12/5; 'when' or 'if' ('which'?) 163/5; 'when, although (that which?), it being the case that' 93/5.

(3) pleonastic 94/2n.

er (2) pres. of **vera (2)**; *era, erat* = *er* + neg. suffix *-a, -at* 'is not' 12/1 22/6 30/5 69/1 124/6 133/4 ('there is no man'); *erusk* = *eru* + suffixed reflexive pron. 'are to each other' 32/2 41/5.

eta (át) *sv.* 'eat' 121/8 151/6; 'cause by eating (*sér* to o-self)' 20/3; pp. *etit* 67/6.

ey *adv.* 'for ever' 16/2 35/3; 'always' 70/3 145/3.

eyra *n.* 'ear' 7/4 ('with his ears').

eyrarúna *f.* 'confidante, close friend, lover (*e-m* of s-one)' 115/7 ('to be your lover').

eyrir *m.* (pl. **aurar**) 'ounce' (unit of weight or value); in pl. 'money, wealth' 75/3.

eyvit *f.* 'nothing'; dat. *eyvitu* ... *því er* 'nothing of what' 28/4; gen. *eyvitar* ... *þess er* 'for nothing that' 94/1.

fá (1) (ð) *wv.* 'colour' 80/5 142/5 144/3; with suffixed 1st pers. pron. *í rúnum fák* 'I apply colour in (engraved) runes' 157/5.

fá (2) (fekk) *sv.* 'get, obtain' with acc. 6/8 130/7, 'receive' 117/9, 'gain, win' 92/3, abs. 92/6; pp. *fengit* 40/2; with gen. 'take' 33/2; *fá e-m e-s* 'provide s-thing for s-one' 106/2, 'bring, cause s-one s-thing' 20/4; *fá sér e-s* 'get o-self s-thing' 52/6; *fá á e-n* 'affect s-one, get a hold over s-one' 93/4,5. Md. imp. with suffixed 2nd pers. pron. *fásktu at e-u* 'provide yourself with s-thing' 116/7.

faðir *m.* (gen. **fǫður**) 'father' 140/3.

faðmr *m.* 'embrace'; *í faðmi e-m* 'in s-one's embrace' 113/6.

fagr *a.* 'fair, beautiful, pleasant'; n. as subst. or adv. 45/4 92/1 130/8; sup. 54/5 91/4.

falla (fell) *sv.* 'fall' 139/6 158/4; pres. p. 86/2.

far *n.* 'vessel, ship' 154/3.

fár (1) *n.* 'mischief, malice' 24/5n 150/2n.

fár (2) *a.* 'few'; acc. pl. m. *fá* 25/6 59/2 62/6; in sg. 'not many, i.e. none at all' 159/6; n. as subst. *fátt* 'little, few things' 103/8 104/3, gen. *fás* 107/3; dat. sg. n. *fá* 'little' 33/6 ('can't ask about anything much'). Cf. **færa**.

fara (fór) *sv.* 'go, travel' 3/6 (pp.) 44/6 47/2 114/6 116/6 155/5 156/5; imp. with suffixed 2nd pers. pron. 119/7; pp. with direct object 'travelled over' 18/3; pp. *farinn* 'gone' or 'overtaken, caught up with' 34/6n.

fastr *a.* 'firm'; (of a promise) 130/9.

fé *n.* 'property, wealth' 58/3 69/5 79/3; 'possessions, riches, money' 92/2; 'cattle' 76/1 77/1; gen. sg. *féar* 39/4 (gen. of respect) 40/1.

feginn *a.* 'happy, pleased (*e-u* with s-thing), glad of, welcoming to' 74/1 128/5 ('do not rejoice in').

fegrst sup. n. of **fagr**.

feita (tt) *wv.* 'fatten' 83/5.

félagi *m.* 'comrade' 52/6.

fengit pp. of **fá (2)**.

fet *n.* 'step, pace'; dat. of extent 'by a foot's pace' 38/3.

fiðr = **finnr**, pres. of **finna**.

fimbulfambi *m.* 'great booby' 103/7.

fimbulljóð *n.* 'mighty song, spell or incantation' 140/1.

fimbulþulr *m.* 'mighty sage' 80/5 142/5n.

fimm *num.* 'five' 51/3 74/6.

fimmti *ord. num.* 'fifth' 150/1.

fimmtándi *ord. num.* 'fifteenth' 160/1.

finna (fann) *sv.* 'find, notice, discover' 24/4 25/4 47/5 64/4 101/4 142/1; with suffixed 1st pers. pron. and suffixed neg. 'I have not found' 39/1; with acc. and inf. *finna e-n sofa* 'find s-one sleeping' 97/2; 'meet, visit, seek out' (object understood) 44/6 119/7.

firar *m. pl.* 'people' 26/6.

firði dat. of **fjǫrðr**.

firna *wv.* 'reproach, blame, condemn, find fault (*e-n e-s* with s-one for s-thing)' 93/1 94/1.

firr *adv. comp.* 'farther away' 34/6.

firrask (ð) *wv. md.* 'hold back from, avoid, reject, go (get) away from (*e-n* s-one)' 162/2.

Fitjungr *m.* 78/2.

Fjalarr *m.* 14/3.

fjall *n.* 'mountain' 3/6 116/5.

fjándi *m.* 'enemy' 127/7.

fjórði *ord. num.* 'fourth' 149/1.

fjórtándi *ord. num.* 'fourteenth' 159/1.

fjǫðr *f.* 'feather' 13/4.

fjǫld *f.* 'multitude'; as obj. of *fara* 'a great deal' 18/3; acc. as adv. 'in numerous ways, of numerous kinds' 74/5.

fjǫlkunnigr *a.* 'skilled in magic' 113/5.

fjǫlkynngi *f.* 'magic, witchcraft' 137/10.

fjǫr *n.* 'life' 58/3.

fjǫrðr *m.* 'fjord'; dat. *firði* 116/5.

fjǫrlag *n.* 'death' 118/5.

fjǫtra (að) *wv.* 'fetter (*e-u* in or by s-thing)' 13/5.

fjǫturr *m.* 'fetter' 149/6.

flár *a.* 'treacherous, false, deceitful, cunning'; n. *flátt* as subst. or adv. 45/5 90/2, sup. 91/5.

fláráðr *a.* 'deceitfully intentioned, deceitfully planning or counselling' 118/4.

flaumslit *n. pl.* 'breaking of happy relationship (*e-m* with s-one)' 121/7.

fleinn *m.* 'shaft, spear' 86/1 150/3.

fleiri *a. comp.* 'more (in number)'; n. as subst. 12/5.

flet *n.* 'boards (of a hall, i.e. the wooden platform or 'benches' used for seating)' 1/7; pl. *á fletjum* i.e. 'in the hall or house' 35/6.

fljóð *n.* 'woman' 79/3 92/3 102/6.

fljúga (fló) *sv.* 'fly'; pres. p. 86/1; with neg. suffix -*a* 150/4.

flóð *n.* 'flood' 137/15 (perhaps referring to the sea, or to a disease, 'the flux').

flot *n.* 'the state of being afloat'; *á floti* 'afloat' 154/3 ('when it is afloat').

flótti *m.* 'flight' 31/2n.

flærð *f.* 'deceit, treachery'; in pl. 102/6.

fold *f.* '(flat) land, field' 137/15 ('earth'?).

fólk *n.* 'host, army of men fighting, battle' 150/3 158/5.

forðum *adv.* 'once (upon a time), formerly, long ago' 47/1.

formælandi *m.* (*pl.* -**endr**) 'supporter, advocate, speaker on one's behalf' 25/6 62/6.

fótr *m.* 'leg' 89/6; *mér af fótum* 'from my legs' 149/6.

frá *prep.* with dat. (postposition) 'from' 99/3 110/5 (see **svíkja**) 156/7.

fram *adv.* 'forward' 1/2; 'on' 79/6; comp. *framarr* 'farther on' (with dat. 'than his weapons', i.e. he should not leave his weapons behind) 38/3.

frami *m.* 'advancement, benefit, profit' 104/5; 'luck' 2/6n; ?'courage, ability, growth, success, fame'? 160/5.

fregna (frá) *sv.* 'ask, enquire' 28/2 63/1; *f. e-n e-s* 'ask s-one about s-thing' 109/3; *f. at e-u* 'ask about s-thing' 33/6; pp. *freginn* 30/5 ('is not questioned').

freista (st) *wv.* 'try, make trial of' (with gen.) 2/6 144/4 (abs.), 'put to the test' 26/6.

fría *wv.* 'woo' 92/6.

friðr *m.* 'peace, truce, quarter' 16/5 127/7; 'affection, friendship' 51/3; 'love' 90/1n.

fróðr (1) *a.* 'wise, well-informed' 14/3 28/1 30/4 31/1; as subst., dat. sg. 'to a wise person' 107/3, partitive gen. 7/6 63/2.

fróðr (2) *a.* 'fruitful, fertile' 141/2n.

frægr *a.* 'famous' 140/2.

frændi *m.* (*pl.* **frændr**) 'kinsman, relative' 69/4 76/2 77/2.

frævask (að) *wv. md.* 'produce seed, be (become) fruitful, fertile' 141/1.

frœkn *a.* 'brave, bold, valiant' 48/1 64/5.

fugl *m.* 'bird' 13/4.

fullr *a.* 'full' (perhaps predicative; *fyr* 'for') 78/1 (i.e. 'I saw their pens were full').

funi *m.* 'flame' 57/3.

fylgja (lgð) *wv.* with dat. 'accompany, be in (a person), be a characteristic (of s-one)' 133/5 ('that there is no fault in him'); 'go with, be part of, belong to' ('constitute, comprise'?) 163/6.

fyr *prep.* (1) with dat., 'before, in front of' 70/6 160/3; 'in the face of' 158/6; 'in the presence of' or 'for the benefit of' 143/2; 'for (the benefit of), in the possession of' 78/2 (see **fullr**). (2) with acc., of time, 'before' 145/7.

fyrðar *m. pl.* 'men' 149/2 159/2; partitive gen. (with *þeim*: 'for those (kind of) people') 54/4.

fyrir (1) *prep.* with dat. (postposition) 'in front of, before' 70/5n; 'in the presence of' 159/3 (with *liði*); 'in the presence of' or 'for (the benefit of)' 143/3,4.

(2) *adv.* 'before, already (when s-one arrives)' 1/7 133/2; 'in advance' 56/5; *nýsask fyrir* = *nýsa fyrir sér* ('ahead of, in front of, around o-self') 7/6.

fyrri *a. comp.* 'former, earlier'; *vera fyrri at e-u* 'be the first to do s-thing, initiate s-thing' 121/7.

færa comp. n. of **fár (2)** as subst., 'less' 12/4.

fǫgnuðr *m.* 'entertainment, pleasant treatment' 130/7.

gá (ð) *wv.* with gen. 'attend to, pay attention to' 114/2.

gagnhollr *a.* 'totally (or mutually) well-disposed, loyal, friendly' 32/2.

gagnvegr *m.* 'direct route' 34/5.

gala (gól) *sv.* 'chant, intone, sing' 149/4 ('I chant such a spell') 152/6 156/4 160/2; pres. p. 'screeching, croaking' 85/4; 'invoke, call up, conjure up' 29/6; *g. e-t e-m* 'produce (increase) s-thing in s-one by incantation' 160/4.

galdr *m.* **(rs)** 'incantation, charm, spell' 152/6.

galli *m.* 'defect, fault, flaw' 133/5.

gamall *a.* 'old'; pl. as subst. *gamlir* 'old men' 134/7.

gaman *n.* 'pleasure, entertainment' 47/6; *mannskis g.* 'the pleasure of anyone's company' 114/5; 'sexual pleasure' 99/6 161/3 ('the pleasure of her love').

gamanrúnar *f. pl.* 'pleasant private intercourse, relationship (*e-m* with s-one)' 120/6 130/6 ('secret love'?).

ganga (gekk) *sv.* 'go' 19/6 38/3 59/3 109/2; 'go on, leave' 35/1; 'walk, walk away' 149/5 157/6; with acc. object 'pass through' ('before one passes on or forward through') 1/2n; 'turn out' 40/6; *g. af* 'leave' 21/3; *g. fram í* 'advance into', i.e. 'increase in' 79/6; *g. um* (= *ganga yfir*?) 'befall, be experienced by' 94/3,

'befall' or 'be current about' (or 'among'?) 28/6n. Pres. p.
gangandi 'wanderer, traveller' 132/7; pp. *genginn* 'departed,
dead' (i.e. 'after his father's death') 72/3.

garðr *m.* 'courtyard, premises' 13/6; pl. 108/3 ('dwelling places').

gátt *f.* 'door-opening'; pl. 1/1.

geð *n.* 'disposition' 6/3 18/4; 'mind' 44/4 53/3; 'mind, wits, sense'
13/3 14/6 17/6n; 'mind', i.e. 'inclination' 12/6 20/2, 'frame of
mind, intention' 46/3; 'inclination, heart' 99/6 161/3.

gefa (gaf) *sv.* 'give' 16/4,6 49/2 52/2 105/1 138/5; imp. 136/4, with
neg. suffix -*at* 'do not give' 127/7; pp. 'given in marriage' 81/4.

gefandi *m.* (*pres. p.*) (pl. -**endr**) 'giver, host' 2/1.

geirr *m.* 'spear' 16/6 38/6 138/4.

geit *f.* (*pl.* **geitr**) '(she-) goat' 36/4.

gel(r) pres. of **gala**.

gestr *m.* 'guest' 2/2 7/1 31/3 32/6 35/2 103/2 132/7 135/5.

geta (gat) *sv.* (1) 'get, obtain' 17/5 44/3 45/3 58/5 65/3 70/3 104/3
140/4; 'get possession of' 112/4 etc. (or 'if you are able, i.e. to
profit by it'?) 162/7; 'receive' 123/3; *ef getr* 'if he can get it'
130/10; *g. sér e-t* 'get s-thing for o-self' 4/5 8/2 76/6; *g. e-m vel*
'provide for (treat) s-one well, be a cause of good to s-one'
135/7; impers. *getr e-m at e-u* 'one is pleased with s-thing,
rejoices in s-thing' 128/7; with inf. 'manage to, be lucky enough
to' 79/2.
(2) with gen. 'speak of, talk about' 103/6.

geyja (gó) *sv.* 'bark at, sneer at, insult'; imp. with neg. suffix -*a*
135/5.

-gi *neg. suffix* (cf. **-ki**) 67/3 139/2.

gildi *n.* 'return, repayment' 145/3.

gína (gein) *sv.* 'open the mouth'; pres. p. 85/3.

ginnregin *n. pl.* 'mighty powers' 80/4 142/6.

gjalda (galt) *sv.* 'give back, pay' (*við e-u* 'in return for s-thing')
42/3 45/6.

gjalti *dat. sg.* 'a panic-stricken person, madman' 129/7n.

gjǫf *f.* 'gift' 42/3 44/5 46/6 48/6 145/3.

gjǫfull *a.* 'liberal (*e-s* of s-thing)' 39/5.

gjǫld *n. pl.* 'repayment, requital, return (*e-s* for s-thing)' 46/6
65/3 117/10.

glaðr *a.* 'merry, happy' 15/4 103/1 (with *skal vera*); n. *glatt* 55/5.

glama *wv.* 'talk noisily' 31/6n.

gleðja (gladda) *wv.* 'gladden'; md. 'make each other glad (*e-u* with,
by means of, i.e. by giving each other s-thing)' 41/2.

glíkr *a.* 'like, similar to' 129/7; 'corresponding to, in accordance
with (*e-u* s-thing)' 46/6.

glissa (t) *wv.* 'mock, sneer' 31/5.

gløggr *a.* 'careful, close, niggardly'; as subst., 'a niggardly person' 48/6.

gnaga (að) *wv.* 'gnaw' 106/3.

gnapa (ð) *wv.* 'reach, stretch forward' 62/1.

góðr *a.* (*n.* **gott**) 'good' 4/4 34/4 101/5 102/1 108/5 120/5 123/4 130/5 133/4 134/7; 'kind' 117/10; *g. e-m* 'beneficial to s-one' 12/1,2 112/4 etc. (i.e. *ráð* n. pl.) 162/7 (i.e. *ljóð*); *g. e-s* 'liberal of s-thing' 39/2 ('hospitable'); acc. m. as subst. 'a good one' 61/7 (*hest*) 76/6 (*orðstír*); n. as subst. 'goodness, what is good, s-thing good' 44/3 45/3 103/6n 128/7 130/10, 'kindness' 123/3.

gól p. of **gala**.

gráðugr *a.* 'greedy' 20/1.

gramr *a.* (used as subst.) 'hostile person, enemy' 31/6.

gras *n.* 'grass, pasture' 21/3, 'vegetation' 119/9.

grey *n.* 'female dog' 101/4.

grind *f.* (*pl.* **grindr**) '(cattle- or sheep-) pen' 78/1; '(barred) gate' 135/6.

grjót *n.* 'fragmented rock, (compacted) stones' 106/3.

grunr *m.* 'suspicion'; *e-m er g. at e-u* 's-one is suspicious about s-thing' 46/3.

grœta (tt) *wv.* 'make weep'; pp. 110/6 ('caused G. to be made to weep').

gullinn *a.* 'golden' 105/2.

gumi *m.* 'man' 12/6 13/3 (pl. ?) 14/6 17/6 28/6 (pl. ?) 38/6 (dat.) 53/3 (gen. sg. or pl.) 72/3 94/3 103/1 157/6; nom. pl. *gumnar* 32/1, gen. pl. *gumna* 15/5 18/5 129/8.

Gunnlǫð *f.* 13/6 105/1 108/4 110/6.

gætinn *a.* 'wary, careful' 6/3.

gǫrla *adv.* 'exactly, for certain, quite' 31/4.

gǫrva *adv.* 'fully, carefully' 102/2.

gǫrvallr *a.* 'absolutely all' 146/7.

gøra, gørva (rð) *wv.* 'make' 80/4 94/5 123/5 142/6; 'do, act' 114/1.

há *f.* 'hide, skin' 134/10.

háð *n.* 'scorn, mockery'; *hafa e-n at háði* 'treat s-one with scorn, hold s-one up to derision' 132/5.

háðung *f.* 'insult, disgrace, humiliation' 102/7.

hafa (ð) *wv.* 'have' 49/5 68/5; 'gain possession of' 58/3 99/5 102/9 161/3; 'keep, hold' 64/3; pres. subj. with neg. suffix *-t* 'do not have' 61/7; with suffixed 1st pers. pron. 96/6; 'get' or 'behave' 80/6 ('he will do best'); as aux. with pp. 3/6 9/5 18/3 40/2,5 107/2 110/2, forming pluperfect 67/6 109/7; *h. e-n at e-u* 'hold s-one up to s-thing, make s-one the object of s-thing' 30/2 132/6 (imp. with 2nd pers. pron. suffixed); *h. eptir* 'keep, retain possession of' 105/5. Md. *hafask vel* 'do (feel) well, thrive, flourish' 141/3.

halda (helt) *sv.* 'hold (*á e-u* on to s-thing)'; subj. (optative) with neg. suffix 'let (a man) not hold' 19/1.

haldandi *m.* (*pl.* **-endr**) 'controller, keeper' 29/5.

hálfbrunninn *a.* (*pp*). 'half-burnt' 89/3.

hálfr *a.* 'half' 52/4 53/6n 59/6 ('wealth half belongs to, is half in the power of').

háll *a.* 'slippery' 90/4.

hallr *a.* 'sloping, slanting, inclined' 52/5n.

halr *m.* 'man, person' 20/1 49/6 102/3 118/2 129/9 151/4 158/6; 'a free man' 36/3 37/3 (complement).

haltr *a.* 'lame'; as subst., 'a lame man' 71/1, 'when one is lame' 90/9.

handarvanr *a.* 'lacking hand or arm, one-armed'; as subst., 71/2.

hanga (hekk) *sv.* 'hang' (intrans.) 138/1; pres. *hangir* 134/10; p. subj. 'might hang' 67/4.

hapt *n.* 'fetter, restraint, curb' 148/3n; 'bond, shackle' 149/7.

hár *a.* 'high'; dat. sg. n. *hávu* 119/9, acc. sg. m. *hávan* (with *sal*) 152/2.

hárr *a.* 'grey-haired' 134/5.

hatr *n.* 'hatred' 153/4.

haustgríma *f.* 'autumn night' 74/4.

Hávi *m.* 'the high one, High = Óðinn' 109/3,4 111/9,10 164/1,2.

heðinn *m.* 'fur cloak or coat' 73/3.

heill *a.* 'whole, unharmed, healthy, safe' 156/6,7,8; 'sincere, unreserved, genuine' 105/6; *illa h.* 'in bad health' 69/2. In greeting, 'hail to', 'blessed be', 'good wishes to' 2/1 164/5,6,8.

heilla (að) *wv.* 'bewitch, put a spell on'; subj. 129/9.

heilyndi *n.* 'health' 68/4.

heim *adv.* 'home' 21/2 (vb. of motion understood); 'to s-one's house' 67/2.

heima *adv.* 'at home' 5/3 36/3 37/3 83/5 103/1.

heimhamr *m.* 'home shape, proper shape' 155/6n.

heimhugr *m.* 'home thought, proper thought' 155/7n (i.e. 'they are confused').

heimisgarðar *m. pl.* 'courtyards of a house, homestead(s), premises' 6/5.

heimskr *a.* 'foolish' 20/6 94/4 (predicative, 'makes into fools'); as subst. 93/5.

heimta (mt) *wv.* 'claim'; *h. aptr* 'recover possession of' or 'take back home' 14/5.

heipt *f.* 'fury, hatred'; gen. pl. 151/5; dat. pl. 'with, for, in case of hatreds' 137/12.

heiptmǫgr *m.* 'person of hatred, enemy' 148/3.

heita (hét) *sv.* (1) 'be called' 13/1 103/7 146/4 (usually after the name); pp. (*vera* understood) 63/3.
(2) *h. e-u* 'promise s-thing' 130/8 ('promise fair', 'make fair promises').

heitr *a.* 'hot'; comp. with dat. 'hotter than' 51/1.

heldr *adv. comp.* (*conj.*) '(but) rather, instead' 6/3; *h. en* 'rather than, instead of' 151/6; *in heldr* 'either (any more than them)' 61/6; *at heldr* 'the more (in spite of that)' 96/6.

henda (nd) *wv.* '(try to) get (catch) hold of' 90/9.

hér *adv.* 'here' 67/1.

herr *m.* (*pl.* **herjar**) 'harrier, destroyer' 73/1.

hestr *m.* 'horse' 61/6 83/5 89/4.

heyra (ð) *wv.* 'hear'; with inf. 'hear (s-one, people) doing s-thing, hear s-thing being done' 111/7,11.

hildingr *m.* 'warrior' or 'prince' 153/5.

hildr *f.* 'battle' 156/6,7.

hindri *a. comp.* 'following' 109/1.

hinn *pron.* 'that one (in contrast)'; *hinn (...) er* 'that one (...) who' 8/1 27/8 75/1; n. *hitt* 'this on the other hand' 99/4.

hitta (tt) *wv.* 'hit' 66/6.

hittki = *hitt* (n. of **hinn**) 'that on the contrary' + neg. suffix *-gi*, 'not'; *h. ... at* 22/4, *h. ... þótt* 24/4, *h. ... hvat* 26/4.

hjálp *f.* 'help, salvation' 146/4.

hjálpa (halp) *sv.* 'help, save (*e-m við e-u* s-one from, against s-thing)' 146/5.

hjarta *n.* 'heart' 37/4 55/4 95/2 96/4 121/8; pl. 84/5.

hjǫrð *f.* 'herd, flock' 21/1 71/2.

hjǫrr *m.* 'sword' 158/6.

hlátr *m.* (*dat.* **hlátri**) '(scornful) laughter' 42/4 132/5.

hleifr *m.* 'loaf' 52/4 139/1.

hlíf *f.* 'protection' 82/6.

hljóð *n.* 'hearing' 7/3n (dat. 'with his hearing').

hlýða (dd) *wv.* 'listen (*á e-t* to s-thing, *e-u* with s-thing)' 7/4 111/6 164/8.

hlýja *wv.* with dat. 'protect'; 3rd pers. sg. with suffixed neg. 50/3.

hlæja (hló) *sv.* 'laugh (*at e-u, e-m* at s-thing, s-one)' 22/3; imp. with suffixed 2nd pers. pron. 134/6; *h. við e-m* 'smile at s-one, laugh pleasantly with s-one' 46/4.

hlœgi *n.* 'laughter, ridicule' 20/4.

hníga (hné) *sv.* 'sink down'; 'fall (in battle)' 158/6 (with neg. suffix).

hóf *n.* 'moderation, due amount'; *at hófi* 'in accordance with what is proper' 19/2n; *í hófi* 'within bounds' 64/3.

hold *n.* 'flesh' 96/4.

horn *n.* '(drinking) horn'; dat. with neg. suffix *-gi* 'no, any horn' 139/2.

horskr *a.* 'wise, sensible' 63/3 91/6 96/5 102/8; as subst., 'a wise person, man' 6/4 20/5 (pl.) 93/4 94/4.

hotvetna *pron. n.* 'everything whatever, all kinds of things' 48/5. Cf. **hvívetna**.

hraðmæltr *a.* 'fast in speech, fast talking' 29/4.

hreinn *m.* 'reindeer' 90/10.

hrekja (hrakða) *wv.* 'drive away' 135/6 (optative).

hrímþurs *m.* 'frost-giant' 109/2.

hringleginn *a.* (*pp.*) 'lying in a ring, coiled' 86/4.

hrís *n.* 'brushwood' 119/8.

Hroptatýr *m.* 160/6n.

Hroptr *m.* 142/7n.

hross *n.* 'horse' 71/1.

hrœsinn *a.* 'boastful (*at e-u* about or in s-thing)' 6/2n.

hrørna (að) *wv.* 'wither, decay' 50/1.

hugall *a.* 'thoughtful' 15/1.

hugbrigðr *a.* 'changeable in mind, fickle (*við e-n* towards s-one)' 102/3.

hugr *m.* 'thought, feelings' 91/3 95/1 105/6 117/10 ('opinion'? 'intention'?) 121/10 124/3; acc. pl. *hugi* 91/6 161/4; *mæla um hug* 'speak around (other than, contrary to) what one thinks' 46/5.

hundr *m.* 'dog' 83/6.

hús *n.* 'house' 89/3.

hvaðan *adv.* 'from anywhere, from everywhere' 156/8.

hvar *adv.* 'where' 1/6; 'everywhere'; *hér ok hvar* 'here and there, in various places' 67/1; interrog. 2/3.

hvárr *pron. a.* 'each (of two)' 53/6n; with partitive gen. 88/6.

hvars = *hvar er* 'wherever' 127/5 137/5 153/4.

hvat *pron.* 'what' 26/5; 'everything whatever' 5/3; interrog. '(why or) how' 50/6n 110/3.

hvatr *a.* 'keen, active'; as subst. 59/6, sup. 64/6.

hvé *adv.* 'how' 144/1-8.

hveim *pron. a. dat.* 'for any' 95/5; *h. er* 'for anyone who, for whoever' 76/6.

hvél *n.* 'wheel' 84/4.

hverfa (1) (hvarf) *sv.* 'turn' (intrans.), 'revolve'; pres. p. 'turning' 84/4; '(re)turn' 99/1.

hverfa (2) (ð) *wv.* 'make turn'; *h. hugi e-m* 'turn (change) s-one's thoughts or feelings (or mind?)' 161/4.

hverfr *a.* 'changeable' 74/4.

hverr *pron. a.* (*acc.* **hvern**) (1) 'each, every' 14/6 37/6 73/3; 'every (kind of)' 102/7 136/6; 'each one, each person, everyone' 36/3 37/3 77/6; with partitive gen. 'every' 7/6 15/5 18/5 54/2 55/2 56/2 63/2 64/2; *h. er* 'whoever'; *þá ... h. er* i.e. 'whenever s-one' 124/2.
(2) 'which, what' 18/4 133/3; *hvers* 'of what (kind?)' 138/9n ('from what (kind of) roots'). Cf. **hvat, hveim.**

hvítarmr *a.* 'white-armed' 161/5.

hvívetna *pron. n. dat.* (of **hotvetna**) 'everything whatsoever, all kinds of things' 22/3 23/3.

hyggja (1) *f.* 'understanding, intelligence, intellect' 160/6.

hyggja (2) (hugða) *wv.* 'think'; with suffixed 1st pers. pron. *-k* 111/5; with acc. object *h. flátt* 'think deceitful thoughts' 45/5 90/2 91/5 ('when we are thinking most deceitful thoughts'); with acc. and inf. 24/2 25/2; with *at*-clause 110/2, 'expect, intend' 99/4; *h. at e-u* 'think about, ponder over s-thing' 23/3; pp. *hugat* 'intended (*e-m* for s-one)' 40/5. Md. with inf. *hyggjask munu* 'think that one will' 16/2.

hyggjandi *f.* 'thought, intellect, mind' 6/1n.

hýróg *n.* 'household strife' 137/11.

hæðinn *a.* 'mocking, scornful (*at e-m* of s-one)' 31/3.

hætta (tt) *wv.* 'risk (*e-u til* s-thing for it)' 106/6.

hættr *a.* 'at risk' 88/6.

hǫfuð *n.* 'head'; i.e. 'life' 106/6; *hǫfuðs bani* 'a man's complete destruction' (but in this context perhaps literal) 73/2.

hǫgg *n.* 'blow' 82/7.

hǫggva (hjó) *sv.* 'cut (down)' 82/1.

hǫlðr *m.* 'free farmer; man' 42/5 94/5.

hǫll *f.* 'hall' 137/11n; dat. *hǫllu* 109/4 111/9,10 164/2.

hǫnd *f.* 'hand, arm' 73/4 149/7.

í *prep.* (1) with acc. 'to' 66/2,3; 'into, on to' 66/6; 'into' 79/6 84/6 158/5; 'in (from in)' 73/3; 'to (bring about)' 104/5; (of time) 'at'

37/6. (2) with dat. (of place) 'in' 10/5 13/6 35/3 96/2 104/6
113/6 129/6 150/3 157/5, postposition 8/6 ('dependent on')
109/4 111/10 164/2, 'on' 90/10; (of time) 'in' 26/3·(place?)
) 82/1 (to be understood also in lines 2 and 3) 90/7; (abstract) 'with, by means of' 52/3, 'in' (manner) 64/3.

iðgjǫld *n. pl.* 'return, recompense (*e-s* for s-thing)' 105/4.

ifi *m.* 'doubt'; *ifi er mér á* 'I am doubtful about it' 108/1.

illa *adv.* 'badly' 69/2 (see **heill**) 126/8; 'not well' 45/2 46/2; 'incompletely, inadequately' 90/6; with dat. 'badly off (in s-thing), having a bad (s-thing)' 22/2 ('with an evil disposition').

illr *a.* 'bad' 9/4 34/2 51/2 105/4 117/5,8 118/3 123/1 133/6; dat. sg. n. as subst. 'with evil' 128/5.

in *adv.* pleonastic with comp. 61/6.

inn (1) *adv.* 'in' 2/2 3/2.

inn (2) (*n.* **it**) *art.* 'the'; usually with a. and subst. 7/1 14/3 67/5 92/5 96/5 100/2 101/5 102/5,8 104/1 105/3 108/5 117/10 140/2,5 161/2 162/3; with comp. a. and subst. 109/1; with subst. preceding 80/3; with a. used as subst. *it sama* 28/3 76/3 77/3, with comp. a. used as subst. 125/7,8, with ord. num. used as subst. 51/5; combined with another pron. for emphasis *sá inn* with a. and subst. 94/6, *síns ins* with a. and subst. 105/6,7, *þat (...) it* with ord. num. used as subst. 131/9 ('this third thing') 148/1–163/1 ('this third one', i.e. *ljóð* etc.).

innan *adv.* 'from inside' 112/7.

inni *adv.* 'inside' 133/2.

íss *m.* 'ice' 81/5 83/2 86/3 90/4.

jaðarr *m.* 'rim, edge' 107/6n.

jafnspakr *a.* 'equally wise' 53/5.

jarl *m.* 'earl, ruler next in rank to a king' 97/4.

jór *m.* 'horse' 89/5 90/3.

jǫrð *f.* 'earth' 137/6,7.

jǫtunn *m.* 'giant' 104/1 106/5 108/3 143/4 164/4.

-k *1st pers. pron.* suffixed to vbs. 'I' 67/3 96/3 ?106/2n ?108/6n 111/4,5 112/1–137/1 154/6 157/5; pleonastic 13/5 39/1 (+ neg. suffix *-a*) 96/6 108/4 150/6 155/4 163/2; combined with neg. suffix and doubled 150/5 (*stǫðva + ek + a + ek*) 152/5 (*bjarga + ek + a + ek*) after separate *ek*.

kala (kól) *sv.* 'be (become) cold, freeze'; pp. *kalinn á kné* 'with cold knees' 3/3.

kálfr *m.* 'calf' 87/1.

kanna (að) *wv.* 'explore, make trial of, get to know' 102/2 ('if one examines (them, it) carefully').

karl *m.* 'man, male' 91/3.

katli dat. sg. of **ketill**.

kaupa (keypta) *wv.* 'buy, obtain by exchange' 83/3; *kaupir sér e-t í e-u* 'one buys s-thing for o-self with, in exchange for s-thing' 52/3; pp. *keyptr* 'bought' or 'exchanged' 107/1n ('which was a good bargain').

kenna (d) *wv.* 'teach (*e-m* to s-one)'; with suffixed 1st pers. pron. 163/2.

ker *n.* 'goblet, cup, bowl' 19/1 52/5.

ketill *m.* 'kettle'; dat. sg. *katli* 85/8.

-ki (= **-gi**) *neg. suffix* 22/4 24/4 26/4.

kjósa (kaus) *sv.* 'choose (*e-m* for s-one)' 137/6 (imp.).

kné *n.* 'knee' 3/3.

koma (kom) *sv.* (*pres.* **kømr**) 'come' 4/2 6/5 7/2 17/2 20/5 27/2 30/3 33/3 51/5 62/2 64/5 66/2 98/2 100/1 134/9 145/9 156/8 158/5; 'arrive' 133/3; impers. *er yfir kømr* 'when one has got across it' 81/5; *er at e-u kømr* 'when s-thing comes' 23/5 25/5n; pp. 2/2 3/2 101/2 104/2 107/5 108/2 109/6.

kona *f.* (*gen. pl.* **kvenna**) 'woman' 81/2 ('wife'?) 84/3 ('wife'?) 90/1 91/3 101/5 108/5 113/5 118/3 130/5 161/5; 'wife' 115/5 131/8 146/2 163/3.

konungr *m.* 'king' 86/8.

kópa (ð) *wv.* 'stare' 17/1.

koss *m.* 'kiss' 82/8.

kráka *f.* 'crow' 85/4.

kú acc. of **kýr**.

kuðr *a.* 'wise' 57/5n.

kunna (kann, kunna) *pret. pres. vb.* 'know (how to do s-thing)' 28/2 33/6; 'be able to' 103/8; *k. svá* 'be able to do that, have such knowledge or ability' 159/6; 'know, understand' 5/5 21/5 27/5 60/3 146/1 147/1–163/1, with neg. suffix *-at* 146/2; with object understood (*mál*) 164/6; 'know about' 163/5; 'know of, perceive, know (s-thing) to be' 127/5; *k. skil e-s* 'know details of s-thing' 159/5; with *at* and inf. 'know how to, be able to' 152/6.

kveða (kvað) *sv.* 'say' 84/3 134/7; with a., 'say s-thing is s-thing' 12/2 ('as they say it is good'); 'speak, utter, recite, perform' 164/1,5; *k. við* 'say in reply' 26/5; imp. with 2nd pers. pron. suffixed 127/6n (*k. e-t at e-u* 'account s-thing to s-thing, declare s-thing as (to be) s-thing').

kveðja (kvadda) *wv.* 'call (on, to)'; *k. e-n at e-u* 'appeal to s-one for s-thing, persuade s-one to s-thing' 130/6; *k. e-t e-u* 'invoke s-thing for s-thing' 137/12; *k. e-n e-s* 'call forth s-thing from s-one, provoke s-one to s-thing' 151/5.

kveld *n.* 'evening, nightfall' 81/1.

kvenna gen. pl. of **kona**.

kveykja (kt) *wv.* 'kindle'; md. 'catch fire' 57/3.

kvikr *a.* 'alive'; as subst., 'a living person' 70/3.

kyn *n.* 'kind, origin, nature'; *hvers kyns* 'of what kind (kin?)' 133/3.

kynni *n.* 'visit to an acquaintance' 17/2 30/3 33/3.

kýr *f.* 'cow'; acc. *kú* 70/3.

kyrra (ð) *wv.* 'calm, quieten' 154/4.

kømr pres. of **koma**.

langvinr *a.* 'long-standing friend, old friend' 156/3.

láta (lét) *sv.* (1) with acc. and inf. 'cause, let, make s-one (to) do s-thing' 105/5 ('I left her with'); 'allow' 117/6 (imp. with 2nd pers. pron. suffixed); *létumk fá* 'I caused (Rati's mouth) to provide for me' (md.) or 'I caused (it) to provide' (suffixed 1st pers. pron. -*k*) 106/2n; with acc. understood 130/9 ('let it (the promise) be firm').

(2) with acc. and pp. 'cause s-one to be s-thing' 110/5 ('caused S. to be cheated and G. to be grieved'); with pp. in an impers. expression 128/7 ('let yourself be pleased, take pleasure', see **geta**).

(3) *l. sem* 'behave as though' 33/5.

laun *n. pl.* 'reward, recompense, repayment' 39/6 123/3 (*e-s* for s-thing).

lausung *f.* 'deception, falsehood' 42/6 45/6.

leggja (lagða) *wv.* 'lay'; *lǫgðumk yfir* = *lagði yfir mik* or *lagða ek yfir* 108/6n; pp. *lagit* 'laid, placed' 84/6.

leiða (dd) *wv.* 'lead, take, accompany, conduct' 156/3.

leiðask (dd) *wv. md.* 'hate, take a dislike to' 130/10.

leiðr *a.* 'loathed, hateful, unwelcome' 39/6; as subst., 'a hated, unwelcome person' 35/4 40/4 66/6.

leika (lék) *sv.* 'play, move to and fro, dance' 155/3; 'deceive, outwit, make a fool of (you)' 131/10.

leikr *m.* 'play, game' 86/7.

leita (að) *wv.* 'seek (*e-m e-s* s-thing for s-one)' 112/7 (*l. út* 'go out to find'), 'try to cause (s-one s-thing)' 102/8, 'seek (and find), fetch (s-thing for s-one)' 141/5,7.

lengi *adv.* 'for a long time' 35/5 50/6 162/6 (i.e. 'for ever'?); sup. *lengst* 'for the longest time, for a very long time' 41/5.

lesa (las) *sv.* 'express; concoct?' 24/5n.

leyfa (ð) *wv.* 'praise' 81/1 92/4.

leyna (d) *wv.* 'conceal' (with dat.) 28/4.

lið *n.* 'troop, company' (with *fyrir*) 159/2.

liðr *m.* 'joint'; metaphorical ('the right spot (in time)') 66/6n; pl. 'limbs' 113/7; *þér á liðu* 'on to your limbs' 136/6.

lifa (ð) *wv.* 'live' 9/3 16/2 48/2 50/6 54/5 68/6 97/6 120/7; *l. læknar* 'live as physicians' 147/3.

lifðr *a.* 'living, having life'; as subst. 'a living person' 70/1.

liggja (lá) *sv.* 'lie, lead' 34/5; pres. p. 'lying down' 58/4.

lík *n.* 'body' 97/6.

líki *n.* 'body, shape' 92/4.

líknargaldr *m.* 'kindness-spell, merciful charm, mercy' 120/7n.

líknfastr *a.* 'assured of favour' 123/6n.

líknstafr *m.* 'favourable statement, esteem, warm regard' 8/3n.

líta (leit) *sv.* 'look' 129/5.

lítill *a.* (*n.* **lítit**) 'small' 36/2 37/2 53/1,2,3; n. as subst. *í litlu* ('with a small gift') 52/3.

litr *m.* 'appearance, looks' 93/6 107/1n.

ljóð *n.* 'song, incantation, spell' 146/1 162/4 163/6.

ljós *n.* 'light, torch' 100/4.

ljóss *a.* 'bright' 92/5.

ljúfr *a.* 'dear, beloved, welcome'; as subst. 'a beloved person' 35/4 40/5.

Loddfáfnir *m.* 112/1 113/1 115/1–117/1 119/1–122/1 125/1–132/1 134/1 135/1 137/1 162/5.

lof *n.* 'praise' 8/3 9/3 123/6; 'praise' or 'love'? 52/3n.

loga (að) *wv.* 'blaze, burn' 152/2.

logi *m.* 'flame' 85/2.

lok *n. pl.* 'end(ing), conclusion' 163/6.

lopt *n.* 'air, sky' 155/3.

lostfagr *a.* 'delightfully fair, attractive (of beauty that arouses desire)' 93/6.

lygi *f.* 'lie' 42/6 45/6.

lykja (lukða) *wv.* 'enclose (*e-u* in s-thing)' 113/7.

læ *n.* 'destruction, harm, injury' 136/6.

læknir *m.* 'physician' 147/3.

lær *n.* 'ham' 58/5 67/4.

lostr *m.* 'fault, defect' 68/6n; 'evil, wickedness, sin' 98/6.

má pres. of **mega**.

maðr *m.* (**mann-**) 'man, person' 3/5 6/2,8 etc.

magi *m.* 'stomach' 20/6 21/6.

magr *a.* (*acc.* **magran**) 'thin, lean' 83/3 ('when it is thin, in poor condition', i.e. so as to get it cheap).

mál *n.* (1) 'measure' 21/6.

(2) 'period of time, season (three months)' 60/6n (acc. 'for a season').

(3) 'time (to do s-thing)' 111/1; 'meal (-time)' 37/6, dat. pl. with neg. suffix *-gi*, '(at) no meals' 67/3.

(4) 'speech' 57/5 (*at máli* 'in speech' or 'in the course of conversation'?) 111/6; 'speech' or 'business, affairs'? 114/3; pl. 'discourse, sayings' 164/1.

málugr *a.* 'continually talking, communicative, affable' 103/4.

man *n.* 'girl' 82/3 92/5 98/3 102/8 161/2 162/3.

máni *m.* 'moon' 137/12.

manngi *pron.* 'no one' 50/5 (nom.) 71/6 84/2 130/10 138/8; gen. *mannskis* 114/5 ('anyone's') 146/3 ('no one's').

mannvit *n.* 'human intelligence, common sense' 6/9 10/3 11/3 79/5.

mánuðr *m.* 'month' 74/7.

manungr *a.* 'girl-young, girlish' 162/3n.

margfróðr *a.* 'knowledgeable about many things' 103/5.

margr *a.* 'many' 32/1 66/2 82/4 104/4; with sg. subst. 'many a' 94/3 102/1; as subst. 'many a one (person)' 30/4 75/3, pl. 'many people' 62/5; n. *mart* as subst. 'much' 27/6,9 54/6, 'many things' 40/6 59/4.

marr (1) *m.* 'sea' 62/3.

marr (2) *m.* 'horse' 83/3.

matr *m.* 'food' 3/4 37/6 67/3 114/4; gen. of respect 39/2.

máttugr *a.* 'mighty'; weak nom. sg. *mátki* 94/6.

með *prep.* (1) with acc. 'into the company of' 27/2 (though the dat. is used elsewhere with the same meaning).

(2) with dat. 'with, among' 5/6 20/5 24/6 31/6 62/5 64/5 68/2 109/6 134/10,11,12 143/1 153/5; 'between' 51/2; 'accompanied by, having' 156/5; 'carrying' 100/4; 'by means of' 52/4,5.

meðalsnotr *a.* 'moderately wise, clever' 54/1 55/1 56/1.

meðan *conj.* 'while, as long as' 9/3 120/7.

mega (**má, mátta**) *pret. pres. vb.* 'be able, can' 28/5 60/5 (pres. subj.) 123/5 149/5 153/6; p. subj. *mætti* 'could' 4/5.

megin *n.* 'power' 137/6.

meiðr *m.* 'tree' 138/2,7.

mein *n.* 'harm' 151/6 (pl.).

meiri *a. comp.* 'greater'; n. as adv. 'more (in more ways, of more kinds)' 74/7.

metnaðr *m.* 'pride' 79/4.

mettr *a.* 'fed, full' 61/1.

mey acc. and dat. of **mær.**

mikill *a.* 'great' 6/9 10/3 11/3 34/1 148/2; as subst. 'a great deal' 52/1 (i.e. 'a large gift').

mikilsti *adv.* (= *mikils til*) 'all too, much too' 66/1.

mildr *a.* 'liberal, generous, kind' 39/1 48/1.

minn *poss. a.* 'my' 49/1 96/3 104/5 148/3,5 154/3 163/9.

minnigr *a.* 'mindful, having a good memory' 103/4.

misseri *n.* 'season (of six months)' 60/6n (acc. 'for a season').

mjǫðr *m.* 'mead' 19/2 105/3 140/5.

mjǫk *adv.* 'very' 2/4 142/3,4.

mjǫt *n. pl.* or *f.* 'measure' 60/3.

móðr *a.* 'tired' 23/4.

morginn *m.* 'morning' 59/5 (*um morgin* 'throughout the morning'); dat. sg. *morni* 23/5 101/1.

munnr *m.* 'mouth; cutting or biting end of a tool' 106/1.

munr *m.* 'desire, love, lust' 94/6; 'love, loved one' 96/3n.

munu (mun, munda) *pret. pres. vb.* 'shall, will' (future) 16/2 32/5 123/5 136/5 142/1 146/5 162/2; 2nd pers. sg. *mun* 162/5, with suffixed 2nd pers. pron. 'you will' 112/3 etc. 123/2; *munu* 'they (*ráð*) will be' 112/4 etc.; subj. *mynda* 'would' 99/5, *myndi* '(it) would be' 67/2; with neg. suffix *-at* 158/4.

munuð *f.* '(physical) love' 79/3.

myrkr *n.* 'dark(ness)' 82/3 (*í* understood from line 1).

mækir *m.* 'sword' 81/3 83/4; with prep. *á* understood from previous line 82/7.

mæla (t) *wv.* 'speak' 27/6,9 29/1 46/5 91/1,4 92/1 104/5; subj. (optative) *mæli* 'let him speak' 19/3; *m. við e-n* 'speak to s-one' 45/4 157/7; *m. sér e-n* 'win s-one for o-self by talking, woo so as to win s-one' 98/3 (or 'betroth s-one to o-self, come to an agreement to possess s-one'?).

mær *f.* (*acc.* and *dat.* **mey**) 'maiden, virgin' 81/4 82/8 (with prep. *á* understood from line 6) 84/1 (gen. sg.) 102/1 163/3 (dat. sg.); 'girl (daughter or wife)' 96/5 97/1n.

mœta (tt) *wv.* 'meet (*e-m* s-one)' 89/2 ('though one meet him').

mǫgr *m.* 'son' 146/3.

ná (ð) *wv.* with inf. 'manage to, be able to do s-thing' 68/5 121/9; subj. (conditional) 30/6n.

nár *m.* 'corpse' 71/6.

nauðr *f.* 'need, necessity' (with *at* and inf. 'to do s-thing') 154/2.

ne *adv.* 'not' 93/5 108/4 121/9 131/10 133/5 135/5 (combined with neg. suffix *-a*).

né *conj.* 'nor, and not' 50/3 58/6 61/6 84/3 88/3 114/3,5 132/5,7 133/6 135/6 148/6 163/3; without preceding neg., 'but not' 63/5, 'and not' 111/8; negating the preceding as well as following element 126/6n 139/2.

neiss *a.* 'shamed, despised' 49/6.

nema (1) *conj.* 'unless' 20/2 27/6 29/5 33/3 72/6 98/5 112/6 126/7; 'except' 163/7; with inf. 'except, without doing s‑thing' 97/6.

nema (2) (nam) *sv.* 'take, pick (*upp* up)' 139/4,5; 'accept, follow' 112/3 etc., subj. *nemir* 'you should accept' 112/2 etc.; 'learn' 120/7 140/2 153/3 162/8 164/7. With inf. 'begin to' 141/1.

nest *n.* 'provisions for a journey' 74/2.

niðr (1) *m.* 'kinsman, relative' 72/6.

niðr (2) *adv.* 'down, below' 139/3.

níu *num.* 'nine' 138/3 140/1.

níundi *ord. num.* 'ninth' 154/1.

njósn *f.* 'spying'; *á njósn* 'on the watch' 112/6.

njóta (naut; *pres.* **nýtr)** *sv.* with gen. '(get) benefit (from)' 71/6 112/3 etc.; pp. *notit* 107/2; subj. 'let him benefit' 164/7; p. subj. with suffixed 1st pers. pron. *nytak* 108/4 ('if I had not had the help of G.').

nótt (*pl.* **nætr**) *f.* 'night' 23/2 (*um allar nætr* 'throughout whole nights, all night long'), *nætr allar níu* 'through all of nine nights, nine whole nights' 138/3; dat. sg. *nótt* 74/1 112/5 ('at night').

nú *adv.* 'now' 78/3 91/1 104/2 107/5 164/1.

nýfelldr *a.* (*pp.*) 'newly felled, just struck down' 87/4.

nýsa (t) *wv.* 'peer, search, investigate' 139/3. Md. *nýsask fyrir* 'spy (find) things out around o-self' 7/6.

nytak see **njóta**.

nýtr *a.* 'effective, efficient' 100/2; 'useful' 162/8 (n. pl., refers to *ljóð*).

nytsamligr *a.* 'useful, beneficial, advantageous (*e-m* to s-one)' 153/3.

næfr *f.* 'piece of (birch-)bark' 60/2.

nær (1) *conj.* 'when' 38/5; *þat ... nær* 21/2.

nær (2) *prep.* with dat. 'near, close to' (postposition) 72/5 95/2; of time 'towards' 98/1 101/1.

næst *adv.* 'next (time)' 100/1.

nætr pl. of **nótt**.

nøkkviðr *a.* 'naked' 49/6.

óauðigr *a*. 'not wealthy, poor' 75/5.

óbeðit *pp*. (see **biðja**) 'not invoked, not prayed' 145/1 ('it is better that there should be no prayer, it is better the request be not made').

óbrigðr *a*. 'unfailing, reliable'; comp. 6/7.

óbryddr *a*. (*pp*.) 'not ice-spiked, without spikes for ice; without calkins, not roughshod' 90/3.

Óðinn *m*. 98/2 110/1 138/5 (dat.) 143/1.

óðr *a*. 'furious, raging' 90/7.

Óðrerir *m*. 'a vessel, or its contents, the mead' 107/4n 140/6n.

ódæll *a*. 'difficult, troublesome to deal (*við e-t* with s-thing)'; comp. n. as adv. 8/4.

of (1) *pleonastic particle* with vbs. (= **um (2)**) 14/5 67/2 72/2 100/6 109/7 140/4 145/9 150/6.

of (2) *prep*. with acc. 'concerning' 46/1 111/7.

ofarla *adv*. 'high up (*e-m* in s-one)' 118/1n.

ofblótit *pp*. 'excessively sacrificed, too much offered in sacrifice' 145/2 ('than that too much should be offered').

ofdrykkja *f*. 'excessive drinking, overdrinking' 11/6.

ofrǫlvi *a*. 'excessively drunk' 14/2.

ofsóit *pp*. 'excessively immolated' 145/5 ('than that there should be too much immolation')(cf. **sóa**).

ofvarr *a*. 'too cautious, excessively wary' 131/6n.

ógóðr *a*. 'not good'; n. as subst. *ógott* 'evil' 29/6.

ógǫrla *adv*. 'imprecisely, not quite, not for certain' 133/1.

óhapp *n*. 'misfortune' 117/7 (pl.; *at þér* 'befalling you' or 'arising from you'? '(learn) from you'?).

ok *conj*. 'and' 3/3 4/3,6 5/6 etc. Pleonastic, correlative with *ef* 151/4 (introducing the main clause).

ókunnr *a*. 'unknown, strange' 10/5.

ókynni *n*. 'lack of knowledge (of how to behave), ineptitude, bad manners' 19/4.

ólagaðr *pp*. (*laga*) 'not ready, not brewed' 66/5.

ólifðr *a*. 'not having life'; as subst., 'a dead person' 70/2.

óminnishegri *m*. 'heron of forgetfulness' 13/1n.

ónýtr *a*. 'useless' 89/5.

opt *adv*. 'often' 9/5 20/4 29/6 40/4 44/6 52/3 65/3 93/4 133/1 134/7,8; 'generally' 33/2, 'frequently' 103/6 119/7 125/7.

ór *prep*. with dat. 'out of, from' 134/8, postposition 9/6 108/3; 'out of, from being' 94/4.

óra (ð) *wv*. 'show hostility' 32/6.

orð *n*. 'word' 65/1 84/1 104/4 (dat. pl. '(by) using many words')

118/3 122/5 125/5 (as 104/4) 134/9 141/4,5; 'speech, conversation' 4/6.

orðstírr *m.* 'honour, renown, glorious reputation' 76/4.

orka (að) *wv.* 'bring about'; *o. (til) e-s (á) e-t* 'get s-thing from s-thing, make use of s-thing for s-thing, look for s-thing from s-thing' 82/5.

ormr *m.* 'snake' 86/4.

orrosta *f.* 'battle' 129/6 156/2.

ósent *pp.* 'not sent, nothing sent' 145/4 (cf. **senda**).

óskǫp *n. pl.* 'chaos, disorder, monstrosity, calamity' 98/4.

ósnjallr *a.* 'foolish' or 'cowardly' 16/1n 48/4.

ósnotr *a.* 'unwise, foolish' 24/1 25/1 26/1 27/1 79/1; as subst. 'unwise person' 103/9 159/6.

ósviðr, ósvinnr *a.* 'unwise, foolish' 21/4 23/1 122/7.

óvinr *m.* 'enemy' 1/6 43/4.

óvíss *a.* 'uncertain'; *óvíst er at vita* 'one cannot know for certain' 1/5 38/4.

óþarfr *a.* 'not useful, not beneficial, i.e. harmful (*e-m* to s-one)' 164/4.

rá *f.* 'yard (of a mast)' 74/3.

ráð *n.* 'counsel, advice' (pl.) 9/4 112/2 etc.; ? 'situation, circumstances' 109/3n (see **fregna**); ? 'plan', ? 'interpretation' 111/8 (cf. **ráða**).

ráða (réð) *sv.* with dat. 'rule, have power over, control, determine the fate (development) of' 88/4; 'advise' with suffixed 1st pers. pron. 112/1n etc.; 'interpret' 144/2, pp. *ráðinn* 'interpretable, meaningful' 142/2; with inf. 'decide, determine, undertake (to do s-thing), be able (to do s-thing)?' 124/2 ('goes and ... ').

ráðsnotr *a.* 'wise in counsel, prudent'; partitive gen. as subst. 64/2.

ráðspakr *a.* 'wise in counsel' 102/5.

rammr, ramr *a.* 'strong, stout, powerful' 136/1 151/3.

rangr *a.* 'crooked' 126/9.

rata (að) *wv.* 'travel about, rove' 5/2 18/2.

Rati *m.* name of an auger 106/1.

regin *n. pl.* '(divine) powers'; gen. pl. *rǫgna* 142/7n.

reginkunnr *a.* 'of divine origin' 80/3.

reifr *a.* 'cheerful' 15/4 103/2.

reisa (t) *wv.* 'raise, set up' 72/6 (subj.).

reka (rak) *sv.* 'drive' 71/2.

rekkr *m.* 'warrior, champion' 49/4.

renna (rann) *sv.* 'run'; i.e. 'grow, arise' 138/9.

reyna (d) *wv.* 'prove, demonstrate, find out (by experience)' 96/1 102/4; pp. 80/1, 'tried, tested' 81/3.

reyr *n.* or **reyrr** *m.* 'reed, reed-bed' 96/2.

ríða (reið) *sv.* 'ride'; with dat. 71/1; pres. subj. (optative) 'let (a man) ride' 61/2; 'swing, move from side to side' 136/2.

ríki *n.* 'power, rule?' 64/1; *með ríki* i.e. 'victoriously, triumphantly' 156/5.

ript *n.* 'clothing' 49/5.

rísa (reis) *sv.* '(a)rise, get up' 58/1 59/1 145/8; imp. with neg. suffix 112/5.

rísta (reist) *sv.* 'incise, cut, carve' 142/7 143/5 144/1 145/6 157/4.

ro = *eru* 'are' 73/1 133/3; 'there are' 63/6.

róa (rera) *sv.* 'row, go out in a boat' 82/2.

róg *n.* 'strife, discord' 32/4.

rót *f.* 'root' 138/9 151/3.

rótlauss *a.* 'rootless' 85/6.

rúm *n.* 'space' 106/2.

rún *f.* 'secret, secret wisdom, secret writing, rune' 80/2 111/7 137/14 139/4 142/1 157/5.

rýta (tt) *wv.* 'squeal, grunt, roar?' 85/5 (pres. p.).

rǫgna gen. pl. of **regin**.

rǫk *n. pl.* 'fate, history' 145/7n ('before mankind existed').

rǫnd *f.* 'edge, rim (of a shield)' or the shield itself 156/4.

sá (1) p. of **sjá (2)**.

sá (2) *pron.* 'he, that person' 18/6 44/4 75/6 etc.; *þeim* 'for such a one' 56/6; n. *þat* 'this' 41/3n 163/6, referring to pl. subst., 'they' (*trémenn*) 49/4 (with pl. vb.), cf. 136/5n, *þess* 'of them' 60/3; *sá (...) er* 'that person who, he who, the one that' 2/5 9/1 92/6 etc., 'some one whom' 46/1, 'that guest who' 31/5, 'anyone who' 58/2; *era sá vinr ǫðrum er* 'he is not a friend to another who' 124/6; *þeim er* 'for one who' 37/5, *þeir er* 'those who' 133/2, *þeiri einni er* 'to that one alone who' 163/7, with partitive gen. *þeim fyrða ... er* 'for those kinds of men who' 54/4; *þat (...) er*, *því er* 'what' 84/3 95/1 134/7; for *því at* see **því**; see also **þats**, **þeims**, **þeirs**; as demonstrative a. 13/4 19/4 (*þess ... at*) 158/6, separated from noun 152/6 157/6; *sá ... er* 'the ... which' 60/4 136/1, *þau ... er* 'some ... that' 146/1; combined with def. art. for emphasis, *sá inn* 94/6, *þat (ljóð) it* 148/1 etc.; doubled for emphasis *þann hal er ... þann* 151/6; *sá er* as rel. 'who' 3/6, 'which' 50/2 134/10, 'whom' 44/2 50/5, 'those ... who' 147/3, *hverr sá er* 'each (one) who' 63/3, *því er* 'of what' (in apposition to *eyvitu*) 28/6 cf. 94/3; see also **þanns.**

saldrótt *f.* 'hall-band, house-guard' (or 'household'?) 101/3.

salr *m.* 'hall, house not divided into rooms' 36/5 152/3; pl. 'premises' 104/6.

saman *adv.* 'together'; *einn saman* 'on one's own' 47/2, *einir ... saman* 'they only between themselves' 98/6, see **einn.**

samr *a. pron.* 'same'; *it sama* as adv. 'likewise' 28/3 76/3 77/3.

sandr *m.* 'sand' 53/1.

sannr *a.* 'true'; 'just(ified)' 118/6.

saurugr *a.* 'dirty' 83/4 ('when it is dirty'; cf. **magr**).

sé (1) pres. of **sjá (2)** 150/2 152/2 155/2 157/2.

sé (2) subj. of **vera (2)** 34/6 39/6 69/2; with subject omitted 33/5 36/2 37/2 72/2; with neg. suffix *-t* (and pp.) 61/3; *eða ... sé* 'or who was' 163/9, cf. note, conditional 126/9n ('suppose ...'); *ok sé* 'and when it is' 90/6; *en sé* 'than that it should be' 10/3 11/3,6 145/2,5, 'than that one should be' 71/5, 'than it would be' 70/2 124/5; (optative) 'let him be' 54/3 55/3 56/3, 'may they (i.e. *ljóð*) be' 162/7.

sefi *m.* 'mind' 56/6 95/3n 105/7 161/6.

sefr pres. of **sofa.**

segja (sagða) *wv.* 'say (*e-m e-t* s-thing to s-one)' 65/2 111/11 124/6; 'tell' 121/9 124/2; 'give information' 28/3 63/1 103/8.

seinn *a.* 'late, slow'; n. as adv. 'slowly, late, not for a long time' (i.e. 'never') 162/2.

sem *conj.* 'as'; 'the same as' 23/6, 'as though' 33/5; *svá ... sem* 'as ... as' 12/2, 'like' 78/5, 'as if (one were to)' 90/3.

senda (nd) *wv.* 'send' 144/7n.

senn *adv.* 'at the same time'; *allt er senn* 'it all happens at once, together' 17/4.

senna (t) *wv.* 'dispute, contend, quarrel'; *s. þrimr orðum* 'dispute using three words (or more)' 125/5 ('don't waste even three words quarrelling').

sér (1) subj. of **vera (2)**, 2nd pers. sg. 126/7.

sér (2) pres. of **sjá (2)** 145/3.

sér (3) *reflexive pron. dat.* 'for himself' 4/5 8/2 20/3 26/3 37/6 76/6, 'for itself' 29/6, 'for o-self' 52/3; 'to himself, his' 24/2 25/2; *einn sér* 'on his own, by himself' 95/3; *una sér*, see **una.**

sessmǫgr *m.* 'bench-, table-companion' 152/3 ('around (my) table-companions').

sétti *ord. num.* 'sixth' 51/5 151/1.

sextándi *ord. num.* 'sixteenth' 161/1.

síð *adv.* 'late' 66/3 72/2.

síðr *adv. comp.* 'less'; as conj. 'lest' 129/9.

sif *f.* 'affinity' 124/1n.

sigr *m.* (*acc.* **sigr**) 'victory' 58/6.

sik *reflexive pron. acc.*; *um sik* 'about himself' ('in his behaviour'?) 103/3.

sinn *reflexive a.* (*n.* **sitt**) 'his' 2/6 6/1 12/6 14/6 15/6 21/6 38/1 39/4 40/1 42/1 43/1,4 56/4 59/3 64/1 68/4; 'one's' 89/1, 'her' 105/6,7 ('for that ... of hers'), 'their' 155/6,7.

sitja (**sat**) *sv.* 'sit' 2/3 5/6 24/6 33/4 96/2; 'stay put' 35/5; *s. fyrir* 'be present (already)', or 'lie in wait'? 1/7 133/2.

sjá (**1**) *pron.* 'this (person)' 2/3; n. dat. *þessu ǫllu* 'all this' 89/8; gen. pl. *þessa* 'these' 162/4.

sjá (**2**) (**sá**) *sv.* 'see' 111/4,5; with suffixed 1st pers. pron. *sék* 'I see (catch sight of, look at)' 150/6; with acc. and inf. 70/4 118/2 150/2 152/2 155/2 157/2, with acc. and *vera* understood? 78/2; *sjá til e-s* 'look for, expect s-thing' 145/3.

sjaldan *adv.* 'rarely' 6/6 48/3 55/5 58/4 (i.e. 'never') 66/6 72/4.

sjálfr *a. pron.* 'the self, o-self' 76/3 77/3, 'himself' 9/2, 'myself' 143/5, 'themselves', i.e. 'their bodies, their outward appearance' 41/3n; *sjálfum þér* 'for yourself' 126/7; *s. sjálfum mér* 'myself to myself' 138/6.

sjálfráði *a.* 'self-willed, independent, headstrong' 87/2.

sjaundi *ord. num.* 'seventh' 152/1.

sjautjándi *ord. num.* 'seventeenth' 162/1.

sjón *f.* 'sight'; *sjónum* 'by sight, with my eyes' 150/6.

sjór *m.* 'sea' 82/2. Cf. **sær**.

sjúkr *a.* 'sick' 87/1.

skammask (**að**) *wv. md.* with gen. 'be ashamed (of)'; pres. subj. (optative) 'let (no man) be ashamed' 61/5.

skammr *a.* 'short' 74/3.

skap *n.* 'character' 22/2.

skapa (**að**) *wv.* 'shape, create'; *skór er skapaðr illa* '(suppose) the shoe is shaped badly' 126/8n; *e-t er skapað e-m* 's-one's s-thing is made' 84/5.

skapt *n.* 'shaft' 126/9.

skarpr *a.* 'shrivelled, shrunk, withered' 134/8n.

skeptismiðr *m.* 'maker of (spear-)shafts' 126/6.

skíð *n.* 'stick, billet' 60/1.

skil *n. pl.* 'distinction, distinguishing features, details (*e-s* of s-thing)' 159/5.

skilinn *a.* (pp. of *skilja*) 'reasonable, understandable, sensible' 134/9 (cf. *ráðinn* s.v. **ráða**).

skip *n.* 'ship' 74/3 82/5.

skipta (pt) *wv.* with dat. 'exchange (*við* e-n with s-one)' 44/5; *s. orðum* 'bandy words' 122/5.

skjóta (skaut) *sv.* 'shoot'; pp. *skotinn* 150/2 (with *flein*).

skjǫldr *m.* 'shield' 82/6.

skoða (að) *wv.* 'look' 7/5 (*e-u* 'with s-thing'); md. *skoðask um* 'look around (o-self), spy around' 1/3n.

skolla (d) *wv.* 'hover, dangle' 134/11.

skór *m.* 'shoe' 126/8; gen. pl. *skúa* 61/4.

skósmiðr *m.* 'shoemaker' 126/5.

skrá *f.* 'skin, hide, piece of leather' 134/11.

skríða (skreið) *sv.* slide, glide' 83/2.

skriðr *m.* '(swift) movement' 82/5.

skúa see **skór**.

skulu (skal, skylda) *pret. pres. vb.*; *skal* 'shall' 2/3 26/5 50/6, 'one shall' 144/1–8, 'shall one' 110/3, 'must' 63/2 92/1, 'has to' 2/5 8/5 37/5, 'is going to' 136/2; (gnomic) 'shall' 137/15, 'one shall' 137/12, 'should' 42/2 43/2 58/1 59/1 94/2 103/3, 'one should' 35/1 81/1 82/1,5 83/1 103/6; 'ought to' 63/5 (with *vita* in preceding line); *ef ek skal* i.e. 'whenever I' 156/2 158/2 159/2; *skulu* 'should, ought' 41/2, 'should be' 46/6, 'must (go)' 21/2; with neg. suffix, *skala* 'ought, should not' 30/2 35/2 38/2, 'one should not' 52/2; *þú skalt* or *skaltu* with suffixed 2nd pers. pron. 'you shall' 98/2, 'you must' 44/4 45/4 46/4 122/6 130/8; with neg. suffix -*at* and suffixed 2nd pers. pron., *skalattu* 'you shall not' 113/6 125/6 129/6; subj. *skyli* 'should' 15/2 42/5 84/2 93/2, 'ought' 33/2 43/5 64/2, 'should be' 15/5 54/2 55/2 56/2, 'one should' 1/3,4; *eða skyli* 'or (as if) one had to' 90/9; with neg. suffix, *skylit* 'ought not' 6/2, 'should not' 40/3, 'one should not' 75/6.

skyggna (d) *wv.* 'peer, spy'; md. *skyggnask um* 'look round (o-self) carefully' 1/4n.

slíkr *a.* 'such (a)' 98/6; n. *slíkt* as subst. or adv., 'like that' 10/6.

slokna (að) *wv.* 'be extinguished, die away' 51/4.

snapa (ð) *wv.* 'snatch, snap' 62/1 (*á e-t* 'at s-thing').

snemma *adv.* 'early' 19/6 66/1; 'soon' 88/3.

snópa (t) *wv.* 'look round hungrily' 33/4n.

snotr (gen. snotrs) *a.* 'wise, clever' 54/3 55/3,4 56/3 95/5; pl. as subst. 'wise people' 5/6 24/6.

snúa (snera) *sv.* 'turn (to another direction), change (the direction of)', with dat. 161/6.

sóa (ð) *wv.* 'kill, immolate' 144/8; pp. *sóit* with dat. object, 'killed' 109/7.

sofa (svaf) *sv.* 'sleep' 19/6 113/6 114/6; pres. *sefr* 59/5, pres. p. 58/6, pp. *sofinn* 'asleep' 101/3; *finna e-n sofa* 'find s-one asleep' 97/3.

sól *f.* 'sun' 68/3.

sólginn *a.* 'famished' 33/5.

sólhvítr *a.* 'sun-white' 97/3.

sonr *m.* 'son' 12/3 68/2 69/3 72/1 78/2 153/5 164/3,4; dat. sg. *syni* 88/3,5 140/2, nom. pl. *synir* 28/5 129/8 147/2, acc. pl. *sonu* 94/5.

sorg *f.* 'sorrow, grief, care' 121/8 146/6.

sorgafullr *a.* 'full of sorrows, sorrowful' 114/6.

sorgalauss *a.* 'free from sorrows, cares'; sup. 56/6.

sótt *f.* 'sickness, illness' 95/4 137/8.

sótta p. of **sœkja**.

spara (ð) *wv.* 'save (*e-m* for s-one)' 40/4.

spjalla (að) *sv.* 'chat' 82/3.

spretta (spratt) *sv.* 'spring' 149/6.

spyrja (spurða) *wv.* 'ask, enquire (*at e-u, e-m* about s-thing, s-one)' 80/2 109/5 (*ef* 'whether').

staðlausa *f.* 'meaninglessness, nonsense' 29/3n.

staðr *m.* 'place' 10/5 35/3 66/2; *leita sér út staðar* 'go out to find somewhere (to relieve o-self)' 112/7.

stafr *m.* 'stave; runic symbol' 142/2,3,4; 'word, statement' 29/3.

standa (stóð) *sv.* 'stand' 50/2 72/5; *e-t stendr e-n* 's-thing afflicts, lies, comes upon s-one, befalls s-one' 154/2. Md. *yfir ok undir stóðumk = stóðu yfir mér ok undir mér* 106/5.

stela (stal) *sv.* 'steal (*e-u e-n* s-thing from s-one), rob (s-one of s-thing)' 13/3.

stinnr *a.* 'stiff, unbending, strong' 142/4; n. as adv. 'hard, inflexibly' 150/4 ('with such force').

stjórnlauss *a.* 'rudderless' 90/8 (dat. sg. n., *skipi* understood).

stóll *m.* 'seat' 105/2 111/2.

stórr *a.* 'large, mighty' 142/3.

stýra (ð) *wv.* with dat. 'control, have command over, possess' 18/5.

stǫðva (að) *wv.* 'stop' (trans.); with suffixed 1st pers. pron. and neg. suffix and 1st pers. pron. added again 150/5 ('that I do (can) not stop (it)').

sumbl *n.* 'drink' (i.e. the mead) 110/5.

sumr *pron. a.* 'some'; sc. *staði* 66/3, sc. *ǫl* 66/5, sc. *rúnar* 143/5; '(a certain) one' 69/3,4,5,6.

sút *f.* 'sorrow, suffering, anxiety' 48/3 146/7.

Suttungr *m.* 104/6 109/7 110/4.

svá *adv.* 'thus' 7/6 100/6 106/6 145/6, 'so, the same' 50/4 62/4, 'as follows' 111/11, 'that' 159/6; *svá ... sem* 'as ... as' 12/1, 'thus ... as (like)' 78/4 90/1 ('as if one should, it is just like driving'); *svá at* 'so that' 113/7, *svá ... at* 'so ... that' 39/2,5 89/7 133/4,6 150/4 152/4, 'in such a way that' 114/1 149/4 155/4 157/4, 'it being the case that, in such circumstances that' 100/1.

svárr *a.* 'heavy' 105/7.

sverð *n.* 'sword' 86/6.

sviðr, svinnr *a.* 'shrewd, wise' 103/3 (*um sik* 'in his behaviour' or 'concerning himself'?) 161/2.

svíkja (sveik) *sv.* 'betray'; *s. e-n frá e-u* 'cheat s.-one of s-thing' 110/4.

svín *n.* 'pig, boar' 85/5.

svinnr see **sviðr**.

svæfa (ð) *wv.* 'lull to sleep, make still' 154/6 (with suffixed pron. -*k*).

sylgr *m.* 'drink' 17/5.

sýn *f.* 'sight' 68/3n.

syni, synir see **sonr**.

sýnn *a.* 'evident, apparent'; sup. 41/3.

systir *f.* 'sister' 163/9.

sýta (tt) *wv.* 'be anxious or troubled (*við e-u* about, when faced with s-thing)' 48/6.

sæla (d) *wv.* 'bless, cheer' 139/1n (subject 'they' understood).

sæll *a.* 'blessed, happy' 8/1 9/1 69/3.

sælliför *a.* 'having a happy life' 70/2 var.

sær *m.* 'sea, lake' 154/6; gen. sg. *sævar* 62/2, gen. pl. *sæva* 53/2n. Cf. **sjór**.

særa (ð) *wv.* 'wound' 151/2.

sœkja (sótta) *wv.* 'seek, visit, go to see' 104/1.

sǫk *f.* 'cause (of offence)'; 'accusation, guilt' 118/6; '(cause of) dispute, contention, lawsuit?' 146/6.

-t *neg. suffix* with vbs. 6/2 19/1 53/5 61/3,7 75/6 89/7 148/6. Cf. **-a, -at**.

taka (tók) *sv.* 'take (to)' 31/2; 'accept' or 'take up, use (*við e-u* in return for, against s-thing)' 42/5; *t. við e-u* 'receive, absorb, contain, take away s-thing', or 'stand up to, resist s-thing' 137/7,15 ('enclose'?).

tamr *a.* 'tame, tractable'; *illa tamr* 'badly trained' 90/6.

taugreptr *a.* (*pp.*) 'roofed with withies' 36/5.

teitr *a.* 'cheerful'; of a horse, 'frolicsome' 90/5.

telja (talða) *wv.* 'enumerate, list' 159/3.

teygja (gð) *wv.* 'entice, lure, (try to) seduce (*á e-t* into s-thing)'

102/6; imp. with suffixed 2nd pers. pron. 'draw, attract' 115/6, 120/6 (*sér at e-u* 'so as to be one's s-thing, into s-thing with o-self').

tíða (dd) *wv.* impers., *e-n tíðir* with inf. 'one desires, has the inclination to do s-thing' 116/6.

til (1) *prep.* with gen. 'to' 4/2 7/2 17/2 30/3 33/3 62/2 156/2; postposition 6/5 156/6; 'to the house of' 34/2,4; 'for the purpose of, to get' 82/6,8; 'about' 12/6 (see **vita**); as adv. 'for it, on it' 106/6.

til (2) *adv.* 'too' 27/6,9 54/3 55/3 56/3 57/6 61/3 66/3 88/3.

tíundi *ord. num.* 'tenth' 155/1.

tívar *m. pl.* 'gods, divine beings' 159/3.

tólpti *ord. num.* 'twelfth' 157/1.

tré *n.* 'beam' 136/1n; 'tree (used as gallows)' 157/2.

trémaðr *m.* 'wooden man' 49/3n.

troða (trað) *sv.* 'tread (on)' 119/10 (pres. *trøðr*).

trúa (ð) *wv.* with dat. 'trust' 44/2 84/2 ('believe in, put faith in') 88/2 89/8 110/3 119/6, 'have confidence in, rely upon' 74/2; *t. illa* 'mistrust' 45/2 46/2.

tryggð *f.* 'troth' 110/3 (pl.).

tryggr *a.* 'true, trusty, reliable'; gen. sg. (weak) *tryggva* 67/5; 'trusting' 89/7n.

trøðr pres. of **troða**.

tunga *f.* 'tongue' 29/4 73/2 118/4.

túnriða *f.* 'fence-rider, witch' 155/2.

tveir *num.* (*f.* **tvær**, *n.* **tvau**) 'two' 36/4 49/3 67/4; 'two men' 73/1.

tvévetr *a.* 'two winters old' 90/5.

tæla (d) *wv.* 'deceive, delude' 91/6.

ugga (ð) *wv.* 'fear, be afraid of' 48/5.

úlfr *m.* 'wolf' 58/4 85/3.

um (1) *prep.* (1) with acc. 'over' 3/6, 'through' 106/3; 'over, upon' 94/3, 'about, concerning' 24/5 28/6 (or 'upon') 77/6 103/3; 'for, because of' 118/6; 'around' 46/5 (see **hugr**); of time, 'through (-out)' 23/2 59/5.

(2) with dat. 'over' 31/5, 'over, around' 152/3, 'with' 95/3 (with acc.?), 'about' 111/8.

(3) as adv. 'around'; *skoðask um* = *skoða um sik* 1/3, similarly 1/4 17/3.'

um (2) *pleonastic particle* (= **of (1)**) 2/6 4/4 8/2 9/2 17/5 18/3 21/6 29/6 38/6 58/5 59/4 65/3 74/5 84/6 100/3 101/2,3 104/2 105/1 106/2 123/3 129/9 145/6,8 154/2 163/5.

una (ð) *wv.* 'be content'; *una sér e-u* 'be content with s-thing' 95/6.

und *prep.* with dat. 'dependent on, in the hands of' 59/6.

undaðr *a.* (*pp.*) 'wounded (*e-u* with s-thing)' 138/4.

undir *prep.* with (-dat. or) acc. 'under' 156/4; as adv. 'beneath' 106/4, see **standa**.

ungr *a.* 'young' 47/1 158/2.

unna (**ann, unna**) *pret. pres. vb.* with dat. 'love' 50/5; abs. 'be in love' 99/2.

unnit pp. of **vinna**.

unz *conj.* 'until' 15/6 57/2.

upp *adv.* 'up' 70/4 107/5 129/5 139/4 145/8.

uppi *adv.* 'up' 157/2; 'displayed, visible', or 'finished, exhausted' 17/6n.

upplok *n.* '(action of) opening'; *ǫllum at upploki* 'in opening to all, to give entrance to all' 136/3.

Urðr *f.* a norn (cf. *urðr m.* 'fate' and OE *wyrd*) 111/3.

urðut 53/5 see **verða**.

út *adv.* 'out, outside'; *leita e-s út* 'go out to look for s-thing' 112/7.

úti *adv.* 'out(side)' 38/5 70/6.

vá (1) (**ð**) *wv.* 'blame (*e-n e-s* s-one for s-thing)' 19/5.

vá (2) *f.* 'misfortune' 75/6; 'woe, calamity', or **vá (3)** *f.* 'corner' 26/3n.

váð *f.* 'cloth'; pl. 'clothes' 3/4 41/1 49/1.

vaða (óð) *sv.* 'rush forward, move fast, fly' 150/3.

váfa (**ð**) *wv.* 'swing to and fro' (intrans.) 134/12 157/3.

vágr *m.* 'wave, sea' 85/7 154/5.

vaka (**ð**) *wv.* 'be awake, stay awake' 23/2.

vakinn *a.* (*pp.*) 'awake' 100/3.

válaðr *a.* 'wretched, needy'; as subst. 'poor person' 10/6 135/7.

valr *m.* 'the fallen in battle' 87/4.

valtr *a.* 'unstable, unreliable'; sup. as subst., with partitive gen. 78/6.

vamm *n.* 'blemish, fault' 22/6.

vánarvǫlr *m.* 'beggar's staff' 78/3n ('to carry a beggar's staff' means 'to be a beggar').

vanr *a.* 'lacking (*e-s* s-thing), free (from s-thing)' 22/6; 'in need of, deprived of' 162/6 ('have to go without'); *e-m er vant e-s* 's-one goes short of s-thing' 107/3 ('a wise man can get anything').

vápn *n.* 'weapon' 38/1 41/1 148/6 (pl.).

vár (1) gen. of **vá (2)** 75/6; (2) pres. of **vá (1)** 19/5.

vara (1) (**að**) *wv.* 'warn'; md. *varask við e-t* 'beware of, avoid s-thing' 16/3.

vara (2) (ð) *wv.* impers. *(e-n) varir* 'one expects' 40/6 ('worse than expected').

vark = *var ek* 13/5.

varr *a.* 'wary' 7/1 131/5, as subst. 'the wary person' 6/6; 'cautious'; sup. *vera varastr við e-t* 'be very wary of s-thing' 131/7.

vatn *n.* 'water' 4/1 158/3.

vaxa (óx) *sv.* 'grow' 141/3, 'increase' 153/4; pres. p. 'rising' 85/7; *e-t vex e-u* 's-thing becomes overgrown with s-thing' 119/8.

vé *n.* 'sanctuary, holy place' 107/6n.

veðr *n.* 'weather' 88/4; *(í) veðri* 'in good weather' 82/2.

vega (vá) *sv.* 'lift, carry, convey', with neg. suffix *-a* 11/5; 'fight' 71/3 125/8 ('attack'? 'strike'?).

vegnest *n.* 'provisions for a journey' 11/4.

vegr *m.* 'way, road' 38/5 119/10; gen. of respect, 'in (my) paths' 47/3; *jǫtna vegir* 'haunts of giants', i.e. 'rocks, mountains' 106/5.

vel *adv.* 'well' 41/6 44/2 61/3 107/1,2 116/7 119/6 135/7 141/3; 'very' or 'moderately, reasonably' 54/6n, 'pretty well, very' 69/6n.

velir pl. of **vǫlr**.

vella (vall) *sv.* 'boil' 85/8 (pres. p.).

velli dat. sg. of **vǫllr**.

vera (1) *f.* 'resort, refuge' 26/3; 'refuge' or '(means of) existence, way (of going on)' 10/6 ('on this depends the poor man's existence').

vera (2) (var) *sv.* 'be' 6/2 15/3 24/2 etc.; 'stay' 35/2; *var mér* 'was to me, for me (my?)' 96/5; imp. *ver þú* 121/6 (*at e-u* 'the cause of s-thing') 131/7, *verðu* 128/6; subj. *sér* 126/7, *þú verir* (optative) 'you should (not) be' 126/5; aux. with pp. (passive) 66/4,5 81/2,3,4,6 84/5 164/1 ('have been'), p. subj. *væra, væri* with pp. of intrans. vb. 'would have' 108/2, 'had' 109/6; *væri þegit* 39/3 see note. See also **er (2)**, **sé (2)**, **ro**.

verða (varð) *sv.* 'become' 14/1,2 35/4 55/5 57/5 75/3 129/8; 'find o-self' 47/3; 'be' 74/1; 'turn out' 41/6; *e-t verðr e-m* 's-thing happens to s-one, befalls s-one' 6/6, 'there comes to be s-thing for s-one' 38/5 ('when there will be') 148/2; p. pl. with neg. suffix *urðut* 'have not turned out to be' 53/5; subj. with neg. suffix *verðit maðr* 'let no man become' 89/7; *v. at e-u* 'become the object of s-thing' 5/4; *v. e-m at e-u* 'cause s-one s-thing' 118/5.

verðr (1) *m.* (*gen. sg.* **verðar**) 'meal' 4/2 7/2 33/1; dat. sg. *verði* 31/5, *virði* 32/3 116/7 (i.e. 'food, provisions').

verðr (2) pres. of **verða**.

verja (varða) *wv.* 'enclose, enfold (*e-u* in s-thing)' 163/8 ('embrace').

verk *n.* 'deed, action, work' 69/6 141/6,7.

verki *m.* 'work' 59/3n.

verpa (varp) *sv.* with dat. 'throw (*á e-n* on to, over s-one)' 158/3.

verr *adv. comp.* 'worse' 40/6.

verri *a. comp.* 'worse' 11/4 95/4 (*e-m* 'for s-one') 125/6 (*e-m* 'than s-one'); *inn verri* as subst. 'the worse person'.

versna (að) *wv.* 'worsen, deteriorate, be spoiled' 51/6.

vesall *a.* 'miserable, wretched' 22/1 69/1.

vex pres. of **vaxa**.

við (1) acc. of **viðr**.

við (2) *prep.* (1) with acc. '(together) with' 44/4 97/6; 'by the side of' 83/1; '(speak) to' 45/4 82/3 122/7 125/6 157/7; 'towards' 32/6 102/3 103/2; 'against, (wary) of' 16/3 131/7,8,9, 'for' 148/3; '(deal) with' 8/4, '(in association) with' 68/6.

(2) with dat. 'at, towards' 46/4, 'in the face of' 48/6, 'against, from' 146/6, 'in return for' 42/3,4,6 (or 'against', see **taka**) 45/6, 'with (by means of)' 139/1,2; *taka við e-u* 137/7,8,9,10,11,13,14,15, see **taka**.

(3) as adv. 'in reply' 26/5.

víða *adv.* 'widely' 5/2 18/2.

viðhlæjandi *m.* (*pl.* **-endr**) 'one who laughs (smiles) at one' 24/3 25/3 ('all those who smile at him, ? laugh with or at him, are his friends').

viðr *m.* (*gen.* **viðar**) 'wood' 60/4 100/5n; 'tree' 82/1 85/6 151/3.

viðra (að) *wv.* 'make weather, be of a certain kind' (of the weather); 'blow' (of the wind)? — *fjǫlð um viðrir* 'there are numerous kinds of weather' or 'the wind changes a lot' 74/5.

viðrgefandi *m.* (*pl.* **-endr**) 'one who gives in return, requiter' 41/4.

víf *n.* 'woman' 102/9.

víg *n.* 'battle' 16/3.

vígdjarfr *a.* 'bold in battle' 15/3.

vígdrótt *f.* 'war-band' 100/3.

víl *n.* 'trouble' 23/6 ('all his trouble is as it was').

vildr *a.* 'wished for, pleasant, agreeable'; n. *vilt* as subst. 'that which is desired, what is pleasant' 124/6.

vili *m.* 'joy, delight'; dat. *vilja* 99/3.

vilja (ld) *wv.* 'want, wish'; with inf. 147/3 161/2, 3rd pers. sg. *vill* 58/2 92/3 103/5, 2nd pers. sg. *vilt* 98/3 130/5, *vill þú* 44/3 (conditional), with suffixed pron. *vildu* 45/3 (conditional); with pp. (*vera* understood) *vill* 'wants to be' 63/3; 2nd pers. sg. with neg. suffix *villat* with direct object, 'will not want' 114/4.

villr *a.* 'wild, astray (*e-s* in relation to, i.e. from s-thing)' 47/3 155/5n.

vilmæli *n.* 'pleasing, beguiling, gratifying speech' 87/3.

vílmǫgr *m.* 'wretch' 134/12.

vílstígr *m.* 'path of wretchedness' 100/6.

vilt (1) *n.* of **vildr** 124/6.

vilt (2) 2nd pers. sg. of **vilja**.

vindr *m.* 'wind' 82/1 154/4.

vindugr *a.* 'windy' 138/2 (weak dat. m.).

vinna (vann, *pp.* **unnit)** *sv.* 'act, perform, achieve, bring it about (that)', with suffixed pron. -*k* 155/4; *v. eið* 'take, swear an oath' 110/2; md. *vinnask* 'last' 60/5.

vinr *m.* 'friend' 6/7 34/2,4 41/2 44/1 51/2 119/5; partitive gen. 78/6; dat. *vin* 42/1 43/1 121/5, *þeim ok þess vin* 'to him and his friend' 43/3; *v. vinar e-s* 'friend of s-one's friend' 43/6; *v. e-m* 'friend to, of s-one' 24/3 (*sér* 'his') 25/3 42/2 43/2 124/6; *erusk vinir* = *eru vinir sér*, 'are each other's friends' 41/5; *at ins tryggva vinar* 'at the faithful friend's (house)' 67/5.

vinskapr *m.* 'friendship' 51/6.

virði see **verðr (1)**.

virgilnár *m.* 'halter-corpse, hanged corpse' 157/3.

víss *a.* 'certain' 99/3.

vit (1) *n.* 'intelligence, sense' 5/1 9/3 88/5; *vitandi vits* 'having good sense, having one's wits about one' 18/6.

vit (2) *n.* 'visit'; *á vit e-s* 'to visit, inspect s-thing' 59/3.

vita (veit, vissa) *pret. pres. vb.* 'know (*e-t* s-thing)' 22/5 26/2 27/8 54/6 63/4 (inf. with *skal*) 63/6 75/2 95/1, 'know about s-thing' 98/5, 'have come, got to know' 91/2; *v. e-t at e-m* 'learn s-thing about (or from?) s-one', or 'experience s-thing at s-one's hands'? 117/7; *v. e-t fyrir* 'have foreknowledge of s-thing', subj. *viti engi fyrir* 'let no one have foreknowledge of' 56/5; with *at*-clause 138/1, *v. þat at* 27/4, *v. hitt at* 22/4, *v. einn at* 77/4 ('one thing of such a kind that, of one thing that it'), *v. hitt hvat* 26/4, *v. hvar, hverju, hvers* 1/5 18/1 133/1 138/8, *v. (þat ...) nær* 21/1 38/4; 2nd pers. sg. with suffixed pron. *veiztu (hvé)* 'do you know (how)' 144/1–8, 'you know, you should know' (equivalent of imp.) 44/1 119/5; with neg. suffix -*a* 75/1, *veita þótt* '(he) does not realise even if' ('does not know but that, whether ... not') 27/7 31/4; with gen., *v. geðs*, also *v. til síns geðs* 'know one's mind, have control over one's mind' 12/4 20/2; pres. p. *vitandi vits* 18/6n see **vit (1)**; pp. *vitaðr* 'allotted, destined, laid down (*e-m* for s-one)' 100/6.

víti *n*. 'penalty, punishment, liability to penalty; injury, misfortune' 6/6n.

vítka (að) *wv*. 'blame (*e-n e-s* s-one for s-thing)' 75/6.

vreka (vrak) *sv*. 'drive'; md. *vrekask* 'quarrel, abuse each other' 32/3.

væða (dd) *wv*. 'clothe' 61/3.

væni *n*. 'expectation'; *e-m er v. e-s* 'one expects, can expect, must be prepared for, s-thing' 73/4.

vætta (tt) *wv*. 'wait for' (with gen.); with suffixed 1st pers. pron., *vættak* 'I waited for' 96/3.

vættki *pron*. 'nothing' 27/8 75/2, 'no creature, no one?' 119/10; with partitive gen. 102/9 (i.e. 'I got her not at all').

vǫllr *m*. (*dat. sg.* **velli**) 'level ground, field, open country' 11/5 38/2 49/2.

vǫlr *m*. 'stave, stick, cudgel'; pl. *velir* 148/6.

vǫlva *f*. 'prophetess, seeress'; gen. sg. *vǫlu* 87/3.

yfir *prep*. with (acc. and) dat. 'over, above' 13/2; as adv. 'over, across (it)' 81/5, 'over' ('whom' or 'me', see note) 108/6, 'above' ('me', see **standa**) 106/4.

ynði *n*. 'pleasure, delight, enjoyment (*e-s* of being s-one)' 97/4.

yrkjandi *m*. (*pl*. **yrkendr**) 'worker, labourer' 59/2.

ýtar *m. pl*. 'men' 28/5 68/2 147/2 164/3.

þá *adv*. 'then' 21/3 47/3 101/4 126/10 141/1; correlative with *er* 23/4 25/4 51/4 64/4 80/1 91/4 96/1 101/3 102/4, with *ef* 17/6 30/4 80/6 89/5; *þá ... hverr er* 124/1 see **hverr**; *þá er* conj. 'when' 6/4 125/8.

þaðan *adv*. 'from there' 139/6.

þáfjall *n*. 'thawing mountain' 90/10.

þagall *a*. 'silent, reserved' 15/1.

þakinn *a*. 'for roofing, roofing-' 60/2n.

þanns = *þann er*, '(one) whom' 45/2 119/6.

þar *adv*. 'there' 104/3; *þar ... er* 'there ... where' 145/8 (or 'there ... when'?).

þarfr *a*. 'needful, useful, beneficial' 162/9 (referring to *ljóð*); n. as subst. 'what is useful' 19/3.

þars *conj*. = *þar er* 'where, when' 67/6.

þats = *þat er* 'that which, what' 40/5.

þegi (1) subj. of **þegja** 19/3 27/3.

þegi (2) subj. of **þiggja** 39/6n.

þegit pp. of **þiggja**.

þegja (þagða) *wv.* 'be silent' 7/3 29/2 80/6 111/8; with suffixed 1st pers. pron. 111/4; subj. *þegi* 27/3, (optative) 'let him be silent' 19/3; pres. p. 'by being silent' 104/3.

þegn *m.* 'thane, warrior, man' 151/2 158/2 (with *á*).

þeims = *þeim er* 'for him who' 3/2.

þeirs = *þeir er* 'they who' 164/8.

þerra *f.* 'towel' 4/3.

þess- see **sjá (1)**.

þeygi *adv.* 'yet not, nevertheless ... not' 96/6 118/6.

þiggja (þá, *pp.* **þegit)** *wv.* 'receive' 9/5, 'accept' 162/9; pres. subj. *þegi* 39/6n; inf. and pp. as subst. (subject and complement) 39/3n ('receiving was accepting s-thing').

þing *n.* '(legal) assembly' 25/5 61/2 114/3.

þinn *poss. a.* 'your' 121/5 127/7.

þjóð *f.* 'people, nation; the people, the public' 63/6; pl. i.e. 'mankind' 145/7.

þjóðann *m.* 'ruler' (of a *þjóð* 'people') 15/2 114/3 146/2.

þjóðlǫð *f.* 'friendly invitation' 4/3n.

Þjóðreyrir *m.* 160/2.

þjófr *m.* 'thief' 131/10.

þó *adv.* 'nevertheless' 19/2 36/6 45/3 162/7.

þola (ð) *wv.* 'suffer, endure' 40/3.

þorp *n.* 'farmstead, hamlet' 50/2n.

þótt *conj.* 'although, even if' 16/6 36/2 37/2 61/3,7 69/2 72/2, 'even though' 34/3,6 89/2 158/5, 'if but' 36/4; after vbs. of perception, 'though, even if' 24/5 ('he does not notice it, even if'), 'but that, whether ... not' 27/9 31/6; 'when' 30/3n.

þrettándi *ord. num.* 'thirteenth' 158/1.

þriði *ord. num.* 'third'; *þat it þriðja at* 'this third thing that' 131/9, *þat ... it þriðja* 'this third one (*ljóð*)' 148/1.

þrír *num.* 'three'; 'three (people)' 63/6; dat. pl. *þrimr* 125/5.

þróask (að) *wv. md.* 'thrive, grow (big), increase (*e-m* in s-one)' 79/4 ('he increases in pride, his pride increases').

þruma (ð) *wv.* 'stand motionless' or 'hover' 13/2; 'remain silent' 17/3, 'sit quiet' 30/6.

þræll *m.* 'slave' 87/2.

þulr *m.* 'sage, seer' 111/2n 134/5.

Þundr *m.* 145/6n.

þunnr *a.* 'thin, stretched (i.e. fine, sensitive), strained' 7/3.

þurfa (þarf, þurfta) *pret. pres. vb.* 'need' 147/2; p. subj. with suffixed 1st pers. pron. 'I needed' 67/3; with inf., p. subj. *þyrfti* 'should, ought' 22/5 ('it would be better for him to know').

þurr *a.* 'dry' 60/1.

þurrfjallr *a.* 'with dry skin' 30/6n (perhaps metaphorical, 'without being caught out').

þvá (þó) *sv.* 'wash'; pp. *þveginn* 61/1.

því at *conj.* 'because,' for' 1/5 6/7 9/4 12/4 38/4 53/4 55/4 84/4 91/2 107/4 117/8 119/8 123/1 137/7; *því ... at* 'in these circumstances ... that' 14/4n ('when it happens that').

þykkja (þótta) *wv.* 'seem, be found to be' 10/5; with inf., *e-t þykkir e-m vera* 's-thing seems to s-one to be, one thinks s-thing is' 97/5. Md. 'think o-self (to be), be thought, seem?' 28/1 30/4 31/1 47/4; *þat þóttusk* 'these thought themselves' 49/4; with inf. 'think that one' 26/2 99/2.

þylja (þulða) *wv.* 'chant, proclaim' 111/1; md. *þylsk um* = *þylr um sik*, 'mumbles to himself' 17/3.

þǫgðu p. of **þegja**.

þǫgull *a.* 'silent'; as subst., 'a silent, reserved person' 6/4.

þǫll *f.* 'pine, fir' 50/1.

þǫrf (1) n. pl. of **þarfr**.

þǫrf (2) *f.* 'need, lack (*e-s* of s-thing)' 40/3; *e-s er (verðr) þ. e-m* 'there is (will be) need of s-thing for s-one, s-one needs (will need) s-thing' 3/1,5 4/1 5/1 38/6; *e-m verðr þ. mikil e-s* 's-one has great need of s-thing' 148/2.

æ *adv.* 'always' 32/5 48/6.

æva *adv.* 'never' 29/2 54/3 55/3 56/3 163/2.

ævagi *adv.* 'never' 21/5.

œði *n.* 'disposition' 4/4n.

œpa (t) *wv.* 'cry (out), scream, shout'; pres. p. 139/5.

œrinn *a.* 'enough, plenty (of)' 69/5, 'only too much (many)' 29/1 (with *stafi*).

ǫðrum dat. of **annarr**.

ǫl *n.* 'ale' 11/6 12/3 66/4 81/6 83/1 131/7 137/5.

ǫld *f.* 'mankind' 32/4; 'class of men'? 53/6n; pl. 'mankind, men' 12/3 27/2 107/6.

ǫlðr *n.* 'ale' 137/7; 'ale-party' 13/2 14/4.

ǫlr *a.* 'drunk (with ale)' 14/1.

ǫrn *m.* 'eagle' 62/3.

øngr *pron. a.* (= **engi**) 'no, not any'; f. *øng* 95/4; dat. sg. n. 'with nothing' 95/6.

ørlǫg *n. pl.* 'fate, destiny' 56/4.